AMERICA COOKS

A CULINARY JOURNEY
FROM COAST TO COAST

Co-ordination of location photography by Hanni Penrose
Food photography by Peter Barry, Jean-Paul Paireault and Neil Sutherland

CLB 2330
© 1989 Colour Library Books Ltd., Godalming, Surrey, England.
Color separation by Hong Kong Graphic Arts Ltd., Hong Kong.
Printed and bound in Italy by New Interlitho.
All rights reserved.
This 1989 edition published by Arch Cape Press, a division of dilithium Press, Ltd.,
distributed by Crown Publishers, Inc., 225 Park Avenue South, New York, New York 10003.
ISBN 0 517 67921 3
h g f e d c b a

Previous page: Fruit Meringue Chantilly

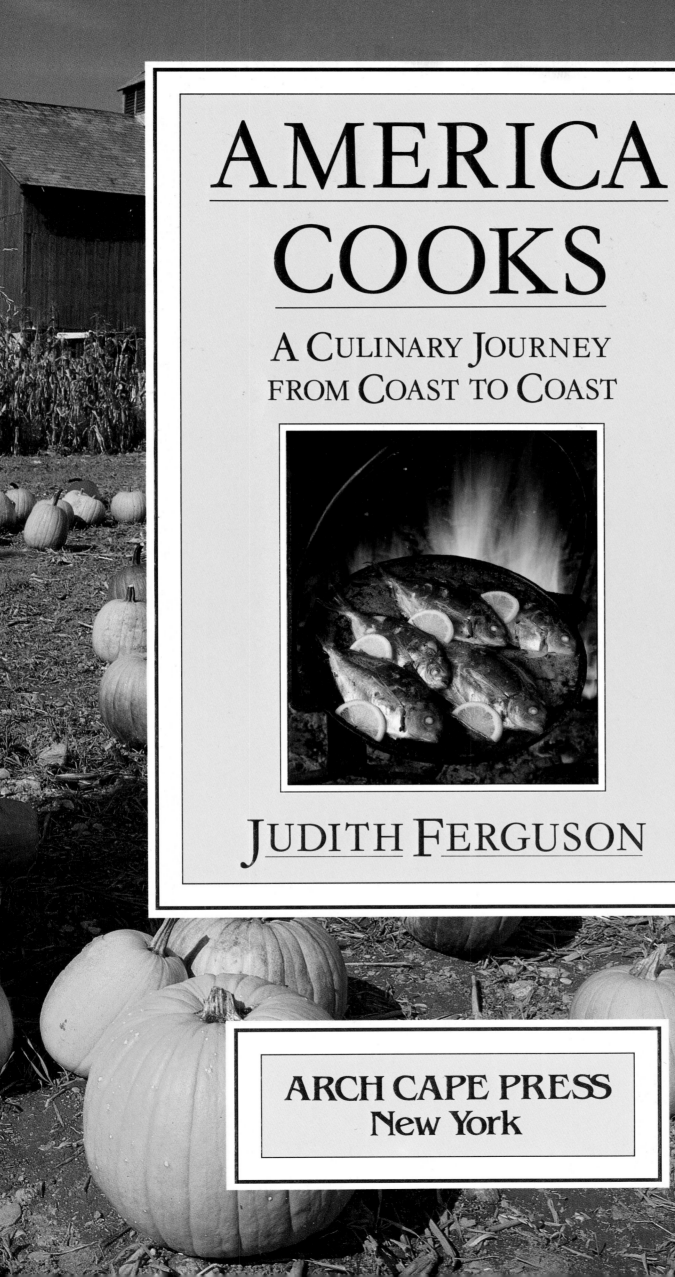

AMERICA COOKS

A CULINARY JOURNEY FROM COAST TO COAST

JUDITH FERGUSON

ARCH CAPE PRESS
New York

CONTENTS

Previous pages: pumpkins ripen in the fall
sunshine in Vermont (main picture), and (inset)
Butter Fish, a Stephen Mack recipe photographed
at his Chase Hill Farm home in coastal Rhode
Island. These pages: Crudité Vegetable
Presentation with New Hampshire Horseradish and
Garlic Dip.

The food of the southwestern and western United States is a mixture too; a colorful one of Mexican, Spanish and American Indian origin. Most of the area that forms the southwestern United States was once part of Mexico and was ceded to our country after the war with Mexico ended. Spanish influence was strong in the area, but the food that has evolved owes just as much to the diet of the native Indians.

Tex-Mex style was born here, a style that has over the years Americanized many favorite Mexican dishes. When we think of Mexican food, something hot immediately springs to mind. But not all the food from this part of the country is packed with fiery chili peppers. Many dishes are a subtle combination of fragrant spices, and are a lot easier on the palate.

Tortillas, flat breads made with different varieties of cornmeal, are a staple here in the Southwest. They appear as an accompaniment to a meal, even breakfast, while also forming the foundation for many delicious appetizers and main courses.

In the western states there is also a good proportion of plain country cooking using fresh local ingredients. There are plenty of meat recipes, for this is cattle raising country, but also some for fresh trout, bass and for seafood from the Gulf of Mexico. Barbecues are a favorite way of cooking here, and everyone has a special sauce used to baste the meat. No discussion of cooking from this part of the country would be complete without mentioning chili. So popular is this soup-stew that contests are held all over the area and fierce debates arise over the best ingredients to include.

California cooking combines elements from the rest of the western states with a bit of the Southwest, a bit of the Orient and a lot of creativity and spontaneity. There is just no stopping Californians from trying something new! The Oriental influence arrived with the Chinese immigrants who came to California attracted by work on building the railroads. Spanish influence was here from the earliest days. There is a Spanish flavor to the architecture, and to the food as well.

The California style of cooking is informal but demands that great care be taken to ensure the appetizing appearance of the finished dish. Tex-Mex cooking is popular here, too, but salads like crab Louis and soups like the famous Cioppino are what classic California cookery is all about.

Vegetables flourish in the Napa and Sonoma valleys. Artichokes and avocados, real California foods that have become popular all over the country, were introduced by Italian settlers. Wine making is extremely important to California and the finished product is highly regarded, even by Europeans used to their own fine wines. In California, the spirit of experimentation and innovation definitely extends to the kitchen.

The Pacific states of Washington, Oregon, Alaska, and Hawaii are all very different and so, too, is their culinary history. Washington and Oregon are wilderness areas, with thickly forested mountains, craggy peaks and raging rivers. They also have extremely sophisticated cities like Seattle and Portland, where the restaurants are as fine as any in the country and the choice of food just as diverse. Mainly, however, these states are a collection of small towns whose livelihoods depend on the sea. Not surprisingly, fish features largely in the area's cuisine, salmon being the most prized. Often served to celebrate the Fourth of July, salmon from the Pacific Northwest is hard to surpass. Oregon is also justly famous for its oysters. Olympia oysters, some of the smallest, are the most highly valued. Delicious apples from Washington are favorites all over the country for pies, sauces, and desserts.

Alaska and Hawaii, the last two states to join the union, could not be more different. Walking along the beach in the tropical paradise that is Hawaii, it must be difficult indeed to imagine what it's like to live in Alaska, where glaciers crash into ice blue water, polar bears lumber across frozen lakes, and snowshoes are standard apparel. Alaska does have beautiful summers, too, but in our mind's eye we always visualize it in deepest winter.

Hearty food was the order of the day during the gold mining days in Alaska. Hungry miners wanted no-nonsense grub and plenty of it. However, tastes in food have changed here as they have all over the country, and a taste for fish has made Alaskan salmon and crab popular everywhere in America.

The Hawaiian Islands are a marvelous mixture of ethic groups – Caucasians, Japanese, Portuguese, Chinese, Korean – and the food is a marvelous mixture, too. Think of Hawaii and you think of tropical fruit like pineapples, papaya, guava, mangoes and bananas. These ingredients appear constantly in Hawaiian food as desserts or as additions to meat and seafood dishes. Pork is the main meat choice and, of course, seafood plays a major part in Hawaiian diets.

The Oriental inflence is strong in Hawaii, and combines with the tropical produce to form a cuisine unlike that in any other part of the country. A luau, the famous Hawaiian feast, is a positive celebration of food during which cooking, eating, dancing and singing go on until the early hours of the morning.

America is indescribably rich in food tradition and history. Our carefully selected recipes capture the vastness of the United States, its natural resources, and ethnic influences. *America Cooks* presents an illustrated journey across our great country. Although we could not stop in every city or village, we hope that you will enjoy visiting your neighbors to the North, South, East, and West. You will recognize both our common heritage and cultural diversity as you sample the delicious easy-to-follow recipes. The essense of the country and its people is so well revealed in traditional recipes. These recipes reflect the history of the country as it was being built and are an immediate indication of the background of the people who helped to build it. The spirit of America is also revealed in the original recipes that evolved from the growth and change of the United States.

As each new group of immigrants came to America during its history they brought their own ways of cooking with them, and their own particular tastes in food have been stamped indelibly on the appetite of the nation. However much trends in eating change, and they have enormously during the last ten years, there are recipes that remain the same and remind us of who we are and where we came from.

Game was plentiful in the thickly forested hills. Settlers from Europe were familiar with cooking game and contributed many a recipe for a rich stew based on venison, rabbit, or game birds. There were wild mushrooms to be gathered and added to omelets and soups just as there were in the Old World. New England contributed much to the country's culinary heritage, and recipes that began here spread down the Eastern Seaboard to other states that were formed from those original thirteen colonies.

The Mid-Atlantic region lies between New England and the South and its food has something in common with both. Philadelphia was of the utmost importance to the development of early America. It was here that the Declaration of Independence was signed and the Constitution drafted. Pennsylvanian recipes range from the sophisticated city food to the basic, simple farm fare of the Amish community in Lancaster County, which has a strong German influence.

New York City probably offers a wider choice of food in one place than anywhere else in the country. The recipes of every ethic group in the nation can be sampled in New York City. Look here, too, for the very best of the new trends in cooking.

From the Delaware and New Jersey shores come an abundance of seafood recipes like crab cakes and stuffed quahog clams. You'll find delicious dishes like oysters casino and baked sea trout, and you can treat yourself to a feast of steamed crabs cooked in a spicy shellfish boil which is very southern in taste.

The southern states are often grouped together as one geographical region, and while it is true that the cooking from this region has a thread of similarity running through it, it also holds very interesting contrasts. On one hand is the gracious style of living that the South is famous for through its history and its present – a picture of elegant plantation houses with cool, shady verandas – ideal settings for a leisurely meal on a hot summer afternoon. On the other hand is its farming heritage, which supplies hearty, unpretentious fare made up of whatever ingredients were on hand, simmered slowly while the work of the day went on.

This area of the United States takes in a lot of territory – down the east coast of the country and around the Gulf of Mexico, along the Mississippi, through the mountains of West Virginia, Arkansas and Tennessee and into the horse-breeding country of Kentucky. French settlers spread their culinary heritage throughout the south, but especially in Louisiana, Mississippi and the Carolinas. Virginia and Georgia share the English heritage that is strong in New England, while the Spanish influence can be tasted in the dishes of Florida. Wherever you go in this region, though, there are familiar foods like biscuits, corn muffins, fried chicken, and country ham that immediately make you feel at home.

The bayou country, those marshy, mysterious backwaters of Louisiana, is home to a kind of cooking that is distinctly southern but also distinctly individual. It's called Cajun.

French settlers expelled from Acadia in Nova Scotia in the 18th century came to this area to join the Spanish and the black slaves already established. The word Acadian became Cajun and a new culture grew, one that was not entirely French, but a colorful mixture. The Cajuns had their own dialect of French and, of course, their own style of cooking.

Their food was based on French country cooking, adapted to the local ingredients. Cajun cooks exchanged ideas with the Spanish, African and West Indian people they met, and these different influences combined with the French influence already there. Wonderful names like gumbo, African for okra, and jambalaya appear in the Cajun culinary repertoire. Seafood figures largely in a Cajun menu, as does the use of hot spices and fiery tabasco sauce. A particular mixture called blackening is often used to give fish, poultry, or meat a crisp, tasty and charred outer coating.

Does Cajun food differ from Creole? The answer is yes and no. Both rely on brown roux, a cooked mixture of flour and oil of varying shades, to give color to sauces and to thicken them. Both are spicy, often very hot and make liberal use of tomatoes, peppers, celery, rice, orkra, and green onions. But some people say that Creole food is sophisticated while Cajun is rustic. It is difficult to capture the essence of Creole and Cajun cooking in words. The ingredients are vibrant and colorful, but not at all unusual. In the hands of these cooks though, they become something special and make both types of cooking unlike any other.

The Midwest is often called the heartland of America. Its climate is similar to that of Northern Europe and it was settled by people from that part of the world. The land was already under cultivation when they arrived. The native Indians were growing corn, squash and pumpkins, and the newcomers began to include these ingredients in their favorite recipes. Because the land was so suitable for farming, agriculture was at least as tempting a prospect as the fur trade, so many of these newcomers settled here to till the land. Later, immigrants from Germany, Scandinavia, Poland, Hungary, and the Slavic countries joined them along with Italians, and the recipes they brought with them were for comforting, nourishing and warming food. This was the kind of food to sustain them through long working days and harsh winters.

They raised dairy cattle in Wisconsin, corn in Kansas and wheat in Nebraska. While farming was and is important, this mixed group of people who became Midwesterners founded great industries and great cities, too, like Chicago. Here you'll find little restaurants in out-of-the-way places that still prepare the recipes our grandparents brought with them. Midwestern cities and their surrounding suburbs have all the diversity you could possibly want when it comes to food. You'll find old-fashioned soups and stews, hearty meat dishes, and traditional desserts.

Pot roast has always been a favorite here and has much in common with the sauerbraten recipes German settlers brought with them. Harvest vegetable soup makes good use of a bumper crop of vegetables from this farming region. Bread pudding is a perfect winter dessert and really warms up supper on a cold evening. Good down-to-earth cooking epitomizes the culinary history of the Midwest.

INTRODUCTION

American cooking is a fascinating subject, but a very misunderstood one. Its image has suffered much from the recent increase in fast food restaurants. Many people think that Americans exist on nothing but hamburgers, milk shakes, and fast fried chicken. They often think that we eat huge portions of food, badly prepared and unimaginatively presented. *America Cooks* presents the glorious food of the United States.

But good cooks all over the United States know better, and they are helping to change opinions about American cuisine. American cooking is as diverse as the people who settled the country. The recipes utilize the variety and bounty of the harvests.

The early Americans, whether they came originally from England, Western Europe, Eastern Europe, Africa, or the Far East, all brought their own culinary heritage with them. Once in their new home, they did the practical thing and adapted those recipes to the local ingredients. Americans, always independent and innovative, are still experimenting with their favorite recipes today. As eating habits and tastes change, recipes are adapted to comply with those changes.

Because convenience is appreciated, more interesting frozen and packaged foods, usually based on dishes everyone already knows and likes, appear on the market all the time. However, tradition is still alive. You have only to look at a typical Thanksgiving dinner menu to know that that's true. Dishes that are cherished all over the country and those passed down through generations are an important part of our national heritage, and are far too special ever to disappear completely from American tables.

To find out more about American cooking you have to look at each region in the country – at its people, its produce, its climate, its landscape and its history. The natural place to start is where the country started – in New England and the original Thirteen Colonies.

Though not all of New England was part of the Thirteen Colonies, it was in Massachusetts that the Pilgrims landed after their long voyage from England, and thus this is one of the important regions in the birth of America.

We learn from our earliest schooldays the important part the provision of food played in the colonization of the New World. The first settlers landed with stores of hardtack (hard biscuits), cheese, beer and dried fish. This was the harsh and restrictive diet that had sustained them on their journey and, naturally anxious for some fresh food, they found the wealth of clams, oysters, and mussels very welcome. They brought seeds with them from the Old World for the crops they were accustomed to growing. When these crops failed and starvation threatened, the settlers had to turn to the crops of the New World to survive. They discovered unusual foods that were destined to become staple crops and favorites of generations of Americans.

The first colonists learned about the local foods from the native Indians. They found out about corn, squash, tomatoes and pumpkins. The Indians had succeeded in domesticating wild turkeys, and introduced the colonists to what was to become the centerpiece of our national feast.

Cranberries, a true North American food, proved to be very versatile. The Indians used this berry as a fabric dye and a poultice for arrow wounds as well as for food. Pilgrim women soon discovered that cranberries brightened up a meal, and they began making sauces, pies, breads and puddings with them. Here were all the makings of the first Thanksgiving dinner – a celebration of hard work and survival. We still enjoy these same foods every year at Thanksgiving.

The English colonists left their stamp on our earliest recipes, giving us the meat pies and steamed puddings still found in our national fare. But immigrants of other nationalities have had just as large an influence on what we eat today. Recipes brought from home were adapted to make use of ingredients available in the new land. For instance, one of the most American of dishes – clam chowder – is said to have French origins. French fishermen used to celebrate the safe return of the fleet by contributing a portion of the catch and cooking it right at the dock in large kettles – *chaudières* – from which the word chowder is derived. The fish was combined with salt pork, onions, potatoes, and milk to make a thick, creamy soup-stew that was a meal in itself. Since clams were cheap and plentiful in this part of the world and available without going to sea, they formed one of the variations that evolved from these dockside soups.

How tomatoes first slipped into clam chowder no one really knows. New Englanders, though, maintain that they don't belong there! Controversy has raged for at least a century over the use of tomatoes in clam chowder. So seriously do New Englanders take the taste and appearance of one of their favorite soups that a bill was even introduced in one of the states' legislatures outlawing the use of tomatoes in this dish.

Seafood played a very important part in the diets of the early settlers. They learned from the Indians how to dig for clams and how to steam them in pits dug on the beach. They built wood fires in these pits, placed on the clams, covered them with seaweed and then blankets weighted down with stones. This was the beginning of the New England clambake. Lobsters were everyday fare, and so cheap and plentiful that hosts often apologized to their guests if this was all there was to eat.

America Cooks

CHAPTER

1

SOUPS AND APPETIZERS

MRS. SAMUEL G. STONEY'S BLACK RIVER PATE

This is an old French Huguenot dish which has been in the Stoney family for generations.

Preparation Time: 45 minutes
Cooking Time: approximately 1 hour

INGREDIENTS

3 parts leftover venison
1 part butter
Coarse black pepper and salt to taste

METHOD

Put the venison through the finest blade of a meat grinder twice. Work the pepper into the butter and add salt to taste. Combine the venison and seasoned butter in a Pyrex dish and pound with a wooden mallet until the pâté forms a solid mass. Smooth the top and bake at 325°F for approximately 1 hour, or until golden brown. Chill before serving.

To serve, cut into thin slices and serve with hominy or salad. The pâté will keep indefinitely in the refrigerator.

MRS. WILLIAM S. POPHAM (NEE STONEY)
CHARLESTON, SC
(FROM "CHARLESTON RECEIPTS,"
COMPILED AND EDITED BY THE JUNIOR
LEAGUE OF CHARLESTON, INC.)

TOMATO CELERY SOUP

The addition of the fresh vegetables makes canned tomato soup taste homemade.

Preparation Time: 15 minutes
Cooking Time: 5 minutes
Serves: 4

INGREDIENTS

1 small onion, chopped
½ cup finely chopped celery
2 tbsps butter
1 10½oz can of tomato soup
1 can water
1 tsp chopped parsley
1 tbsp lemon juice
1 tsp sugar
¼ tsp salt
⅛ tsp pepper

GARNISH

¼ cup unsweetened cream, whipped
Chopped parsley

METHOD

Sauté the onion and celery in the butter, but do not brown. Add the tomato soup, water, parsley, lemon juice, sugar, salt and pepper. Simmer for 5 minutes. The celery will remain crisp. To serve, pour into 4 bowls and top each with a spoonful of unsweetened whipped cream and a sprinkling of chopped parsley.

COURTESY ELIZABETH C. KREMER
FROM THE TRUSTEES HOUSE DAILY
FARE, PLEASANT HILL, KENTUCKY
PLEASANT HILL PRESS, HARRODSBURG,
KENTUCKY 1970 AND 1977

CORNMEAL PANCAKES

Cornmeal, either yellow, white or blue, is an important ingredient in Southwestern recipes. Here it's combined with corn in a light and different kind of appetizer.

Preparation Time: 30 minutes
Cooking Time: 3-4 minutes per pancake
Serves: 4

INGREDIENTS

1 cup yellow cornmeal
1 tbsp flour
1 tsp baking soda
1 tsp salt
2 cups buttermilk
2 eggs, separated
Oil
10oz frozen corn
Red pepper preserves
Green onions, chopped
Sour cream

METHOD

Sift the dry ingredients into a bowl, adding any coarse meal that remains in the strainer. Mix the egg yolks and buttermilk together and gradually beat into the dry ingredients. Cover and leave to stand for at least 15 minutes. Whisk the egg whites until stiff but not dry and fold into the cornmeal mixture.

Lightly grease a frying pan with oil and drop in about 2 tbsps of batter. Sprinkle with the corn and allow to cook until the underside is golden brown. Turn the pancakes and cook the second side until golden. Continue with the remaining batter and corn. Keep the cooked pancakes warm. To serve, place three pancakes on warm side plates. Add a spoonful of sour cream and red pepper preserves to each and sprinkle over finely sliced or shredded green onions.

Facing page: Cream of Pumpkin Soup – delicious and warming fare for the cold November evenings. This page: the placid waters of the Scioto flow past government buildings in Columbus, Ohio.

CREAM OF PUMPKIN SOUP

There are more ways of using a pumpkin than just as a pie filling, and this soup is one of the nicest. For fun, use a hollowed out, well-cleaned pumpkin as a tureen to serve the soup.

Preparation Time: 25 minutes
Cooking Time: 20 minutes
Serves: 4-6

INGREDIENTS

4 tbsps butter
1 large onion, thinly sliced
1 pumpkin, 4-5lbs in weight
Nutmeg
Salt and pepper
1 cup heavy cream

METHOD

Wash and peel the pumpkin, remove the seeds and cut the flesh into cubes with a sharp knife. Set aside. Melt the butter in a large pot and add the onion. Sweat the onion slowly until it is fairly tender. Add the pumpkin chunks and 1 quart of cold water. Season with salt and pepper and a pinch of nutmeg.

Simmer for 20 minutes. Purée the pumpkin mixture in small batches, adding cream to each small batch. Return the soup to the rinsed out pot and reheat gently. Serve hot.

NEW ENGLAND CULINARY INSTITUTE, MONTPELIER, VT

OLD-FASHIONED SPLIT PEA SOUP WITH HAM

This soup is a favorite all over the country, but the addition of a ham bone is particularly New England-style. Garnishes such as crôutons, bacon bits or chopped parsley lend added interest to this soup. The addition of crusty bread and a salad creates a wonderful, hearty repast.

Preparation Time: 30 minutes plus overnight soaking
Cooking Time: 1½-2 hours
Serves: 8

INGREDIENTS

1lb dried, green split peas
2½ quarts water
2lbs ham hocks or a meaty ham bone
¼lb onion, diced
¼lb carrots, peeled and diced
¼lb celery hearts and leaves, finely diced
2 tbsps bacon or pork renderings
2 medium bay leaves
2 whole cloves
3 whole black peppercorns
½ tsp garlic powder
½ tsp thyme
1 tsp Worcestershire sauce

America Cooks

CHAPTER

4

POULTRY
AND GAME

BREASTS OF CHICKEN VICKSBURG

This delicious chicken is sure to be as popular with your guests as it is with the guests at the Magnolia Inn in Vicksburg

Preparation Time: 30 minutes
Cooking Time: 45 minutes
Serves: 6

INGREDIENTS

6 chicken breasts, split and skinned
¼ cup flour
2½ tsps salt
1 tsp paprika
½ cup butter
¼ cup water
2 tsps cornstarch
1½ cups half and half or light cream
¼ cup sherry
1 cup mushrooms, sliced
1 cup Swiss cheese, grated
½ cup fresh parsley, chopped

TO SERVE

6 slices of bread, toasted and with the crusts removed
6 thin slices of cooked ham

METHOD

Coat the chicken pieces with a mixture of the flour, salt and paprika. Melt half of the butter in a heavy skillet with a cover. Lightly brown the chicken in the hot butter, then add the water and simmer the chicken, covered, for 30 minutes, or until tender. Remove the chicken and set aside. Blend ¼ cup of the half and half into cornstarch. Add this to the drippings in the skillet and cook over a low heat, stirring constantly. Gradually add the rest of the half and half and the sherry. Continue cooking and stirring until the sauce is smooth and thickened. Add the grated cheese to the hot sauce and blend until the cheese is melted. Sauté the mushrooms in the remaining butter, drain and add to the sauce. Gently warm the ham slices.

To serve, place the pieces of toast on a large, oblong platter. Top each with a slice of warm ham, then a chicken breast. Cover each serving with the hot sauce. Garnish with chopped parsley and paprika. The serving may also be arranged separately in small individual casserole dishes.

MARTIN LAFFEY,
DELTA POINT RIVER RESTAURANT,
VICKSBURG, MS

BARBECUE CHICKEN

Here is a delicious alternative to Southern Fried Chicken.

Preparation Time: 20 minutes
Cooking Time: 1 hour 20 minutes
Serves: 4

INGREDIENTS

1 fryer chicken (about 2½lbs), cut into pieces
½ cup flour
Salt and pepper

SAUCE

1 medium onion, chopped
2 tbsps vegetable oil

The sternwheeler *Tom Sawyer* (above) on the Mississippi River at St. Louis, Missouri recalls the state's colorful and elegant past. Something of the South's famous hospitality and elegance can be captured in dishes such as Chicken and Dumplings (facing page).

2 tbsps vinegar
2 tbsps brown sugar
¼ cup lemon juice
1 cup ketchup
3 tbsps Worcestershire sauce
½ tbsp prepared mustard
1 cup water
Dash Tabasco sauce

METHOD

Shake the chicken pieces in a paper bag containing the flour, salt and pepper. Brown in a heavy skillet using a small amount of vegetable oil. Drain off any excess oil and place the chicken in a shallow baking pan. Set aside while you prepare the sauce. To make the sauce, brown the onion in the vegetable oil in a heavy skillet. Add the remaining sauce ingredients and simmer for 20 minutes. Pour the sauce over the chicken and bake, uncovered, at 325°F for 1 hour, or until the chicken is tender. Baste frequently with the sauce during the cooking time.

DORIS BELCHER, MEMPHIS, TN

CHICKEN AND DUMPLINGS

Chicken and Dumplings brings all the warmth and friendliness of a Georgia country kitchen home to you.

Preparation Time: 20 minutes
Cooking Time: 2½-3½ hours

Serves: 6-8

INGREDIENTS

1 large boiling hen
4oz butter
Water to cover
Salt and pepper to taste

DUMPLINGS
4 cups plain flour
1½ cups ice water

GARNISH
Fresh or dried parsley

METHOD

Place the hen and the butter in a large pot and pour over water to cover. Boil for 2-3 hours, or until the hen is very tender, adding extra water if necessary. Remove the hen and allow to cool, reserving the broth. When the hen is cool enough to handle, remove the bones, cut the meat into serving-size pieces and return to the broth. To prepare the dumplings, make a well in the middle of the flour. Pour in the ice water and blend with a fork or with your fingers until the dough forms a ball. Roll out thinly and cut into 2-3-inch-wide strips. Bring the chicken and broth to the boil and season to taste with salt and pepper. Slowly drop the dough strips into the broth. Simmer for 2-4 minutes, or until the dumplings are tender. Serve immediately, garnished with dried or fresh parsley.

SARALYN LATHAM, THE WILLIS HOUSE, MILLEDGEVILLE, GA

CHICKEN AND SEAFOOD ROLL-UPS

These are delicious served with a mushroom cream sauce for a special occasion.

Preparation Time: 30 minutes
Cooking Time: 20-25 minutes
Serves: 8

INGREDIENTS

8 chicken breasts, boned
2 cups stuffing, such as seasoned bread or corn bread
crumbs, moistened with stock
1 cup shrimp, cooked and sliced in half
8oz crab meat
1 cup flour, seasoned with salt and pepper
4 eggs, beaten
1 cup milk
12oz butter

METHOD

Combine the stuffing, shrimp and crab meat. Spoon this mixture over the chicken breasts. Roll up the chicken, tucking the ends inside. Dip the rolls first in the beaten eggs, then in flour, then in the milk, then in flour again. Melt the butter in a skillet until bubbling. Gently brown the roll-ups, then drain and place them in an oiled baking pan. Bake at 350°F for 20-25 minutes.

SARALYN LATHAM, THE WILLIS HOUSE,
MILLEDGEVILLE, GA

RIVER INN QUAIL

Definitely a dish for special occasions, this is deceptively simple, impressive and perfect for entertaining.

Preparation Time: 25 minutes
Cooking Time: 45-50 minutes
Serves: 4

INGREDIENTS

12 dressed quail
6 tbsps butter
3 tbsps oil
1 clove garlic, crushed
4oz mushrooms, sliced
4 tbsps chopped pecans or walnuts
4 tbsps raisins
1 cup chicken stock
Salt and pepper
3 tbsps sherry
1 tbsp cornstarch
1 tsp tomato paste (optional)
1 bunch watercress

METHOD

Rub each quail inside and out with butter. Pour the oil into a baking pan large enough to hold the quail comfortably. Cook in a pre-heated 350°F oven for about 25 minutes, uncovered. Remove the pan from the oven and place under a pre-heated broiler to brown the quail. Add garlic, mushrooms, pecans, raisins and stock to the quail. Replace in the oven and continue to cook, uncovered, until the quail are tender — a further 20 minutes. Remove the quail and other ingredients to a serving

Facing page: Chicken and Seafood Roll-Ups.
Below: Broad Street, Charleston, South Carolina.

dish, leaving the pan juices behind. Mix the cornstarch and sherry and add it to the pan, stirring constantly. Place the pan over medium heat and cook until the cornstarch thickens and clears. If the baking pan isn't flameproof, transfer the ingredients to a saucepan before thickening the sauce. Add tomato paste, if necessary, for color. Pour the sauce over the quail and garnish with watercress to serve.

PIGEONS IN WINE

Pigeons are country fare and these are treated in a provincial French manner with the Cajun touch of white, black and red pepper.

Preparation Time: 30 minutes
Cooking Time: 50 minutes-1 hour
Serves: 4

INGREDIENTS

4 pigeons
½ tsp each cayenne, white and black pepper
2 tbsps oil
2 tbsps butter or margarine
12oz button onions
2 sticks celery, sliced
4 carrots, peeled and sliced
4 tbsps flour
1½ cups chicken stock
½ cup dry red wine
4oz button mushrooms, quartered or left whole if small
3oz fresh or frozen lima beans

Below: Pigeons in Wine.

2 tsps tomato paste (optional)
2 tbsps chopped parsley
Pinch salt

METHOD

Wipe the pigeons with a damp cloth and season them inside the cavities with the three kinds of pepper and a pinch of salt. Heat the oil in a heavy-based casserole and add the butter or margarine. Once it is foaming, place in the pigeons, two at a time if necessary, and brown them on all sides, turning them frequently. Remove from the casserole and set them aside. To peel the button onions quickly, trim the root ends slightly and drop the onions into rapidly boiling water. Allow it to come back to the boil for about 1 minute. Transfer to cold water and leave to cool completely. The skins should come off easily. Trim roots completely. Add the onions, celery and carrots to the fat in the casserole and cook for about 5 minutes to brown slightly. Add the flour and cook until golden brown, stirring constantly. Pour in the stock and the wine and stir well. Bring to the boil over high heat until thickened. Stir in the tomato paste, if using, and return the pigeons to the casserole along with any liquid that has accumulated. Partially cover the casserole and simmer gently for about 40-45 minutes, or until the pigeons are tender. Add the mushrooms and lima beans halfway through the cooking time. To serve, skim any excess fat from the surface of the sauce and sprinkle over the chopped parsley.

CHICKEN NUEVA MEXICANA

A very stylish and contemporary dish, this uses ingredients that have always been part of the cuisine of the Southwest.

Preparation Time: 1 hour
Cooking Time: 50 minutes
Serves: 6

INGREDIENTS

6 chicken thighs, skinned and boned
2 tbsps mild chili powder
2 tbsps oil
Juice of 1 lime
Pinch salt
Oil for frying

LIME CREAM SAUCE
¾ cup sour cream or natural yogurt
1 tsp lime juice and grated rind
6 tbsps heavy cream
Salt

CORN CRÊPES
1 cup fine yellow cornmeal
½ cup flour
Pinch salt
1 whole egg and 1 egg yolk
1 tbsp oil or melted butter or margarine
1½ cups milk
Oil for frying

GARDEN SALSA
1 large zucchini
1 large ripe tomato
2 shallots
1 tbsp chopped fresh coriander
Pinch cayenne, pepper and salt
1 tbsp white wine vinegar
3 tbsps oil

AVOCADO AND ORANGE SALAD

2 oranges
1 avocado, peeled and sliced
Juice of 1 lime
Pinch sugar
Pinch coriander
6 tbsps pine nuts, toasted

METHOD

Place the chicken in a shallow dish. Combine the chili powder, oil, lime juice and salt and pour over the chicken. Turn the pieces over and rub the marinade into all the surfaces. Cover and refrigerate for 2 hours. Combine all the ingredients for the Lime Cream Sauce and fold together gently. Cover and leave 2 hours in the refrigerator to thicken. Sift the cornmeal, flour and salt for the crêpes into a bowl or a food processor. Combine the eggs, oil and milk. Make a well in the center of the ingredients in the bowl and pour in the liquid. Stir the liquid ingredients with a wooden spoon to gradually incorporate the dry ingredients. Alternatively, combine all the ingredients in a food processor and process until smooth. Leave the batter to stand for 30 minutes whichever method you choose. Trim the ends of zucchini and cut into small dice. Peel the tomatoes and remove the seeds. Cut the tomato flesh into small dice. Cut the shallots into dice the same size as the zucchini and tomato. Combine the coriander, cayenne pepper, vinegar, oil and salt, mixing very well. Pour over the vegetables and stir to mix. Cover and leave to marinate. Heat a small amount of oil in a large frying pan and place in the chicken in a single layer. Fry quickly to brown both sides. Pour over remaining marinade, cover and cook until tender, about 25 minutes. Heat a small amount of oil in an 8 inch crêpe or frying pan. Wipe out with paper towel and return the pan to the heat until hot. Pour a spoonful of the batter into the pan and swirl to coat the bottom with the mixture. Make sure the edge of each crêpe is irregular. When the edges of each crêpe look pale brown and the top surface begins to bubble, turn the crêpes using a palette knife. Cook the other side. Stack as each is finished. Cover with foil and keep warm in a low oven. Pour about 2 tbsps oil into a small frying pan and when hot add the pine nuts. Cook over moderate heat, stirring constantly until golden brown. Remove and drain on paper towels. Peel and segment the oranges over a bowl to catch the juice. Cut the avocado in half, remove the stone and peel. Cut into thin slices and combine with the orange. Add the remaining ingredients for the salad, except the pine nuts, and toss gently to mix. To assemble, place one corn crêpe on a serving plate. Place one piece of chicken on the lower half of the crêpe, top with a spoonful of Lime Cream Sauce. Place a serving of Garden Salsa and one of Avocado and Orange Salad on either side of the chicken and partially fold the crêpe over the top. Scatter over pine nuts and serve immediately.

VENISON STEW

Preparation Time: 30 minutes
Cooking Time: 2 hours 10 minutes
Serves: 6-8

INGREDIENTS

3lbs venison shoulder or leg, cut into 2 inch pieces
2 cups dry red wine
4 tbsps red wine vinegar
1 bay leaf
2 tsps chopped fresh thyme or 1 tsp dried thyme
6 juniper berries, crushed
3 whole allspice berries
6 black peppercorns
1 clove garlic, crushed
4 tbsps oil
2 carrots, cut into strips
1 onion, thinly sliced
2 sticks celery, cut into strips
8oz mushrooms, sliced
Chopped parsley to garnish

METHOD

Combine the wine, vinegar, bay leaf, thyme, juniper berries, allspice, peppercorns and garlic with the venison, and marinate overnight. Remove the meat from the marinade and pat dry on paper towels. Reserve the marinade for later use.

Left: Bison at Yellowstone National Park's Opalescent Pool, Wyoming.
Below: Venison Stew.

Above: Brunswick Stew.

Facing page: Chicken
with Red Peppers.

8oz salt pork, rinded and cut into ¼ inch dice
3 medium onions, finely chopped
3 pints water
3 14oz cans tomatoes
3 tbsps tomato paste
4oz fresh or frozen lima beans
4oz corn
2 large red peppers, seeded and cut into small dice
3 medium potatoes, peeled and cut into ½ inch cubes
Salt and pepper
1-2 tsps cayenne pepper or tabasco, or to taste
2 tsps Worcester sauce
1 cup red wine

METHOD

Shake the pieces of chicken in the flour in a plastic bag as for Fried Chicken. In a large, deep sauté pan, melt the butter until foaming. Place in the chicken without crowding the pieces and brown over moderately high heat for about 10-12 minutes. Remove the chicken and set it aside. In the same pan, fry the salt pork until the fat is rendered and the dice are crisp. Add the onions and cook over moderate heat for about 10 minutes, or until softened but not browned. Pour the water into a large stock pot or saucepan and spoon in the onions, pork and any meat juices from the pan. Add the chicken, tomatoes and tomato paste. Bring to the boil, reduce the heat and simmer for about 1-1½ hours. Add the lima beans, corn, peppers and potatoes. Add cayenne pepper or tabasco to taste. Add the Worcester sauce and red wine. Cook for a further 30 minutes or until the chicken is tender. Add salt and pepper to taste. The stew should be rather thick, so if there is too much liquid, remove the chicken and vegetables and boil down the liquid to reduce it. If there is not enough liquid, add more water or chicken stock.

CHICKEN WITH RED PEPPERS

Easy as this recipe is, it looks and tastes good enough for guests. The warm taste of roasted red peppers is typically Southwestern.

Preparation Time: 30-40 minutes
Cooking Time: 30 minutes
Serves: 4

INGREDIENTS

4 large red peppers
4 skinned and boned chicken breasts
1½ tbsps oil
Salt and pepper
1 clove garlic, finely chopped
3 tbsps white wine vinegar
2 green onions, finely chopped
Sage leaves for garnish

METHOD

Cut the peppers in half and remove the stems, cores and seeds. Flatten the peppers with the palm of your hand and brush the skin sides lightly with oil. Place the peppers skin side up on the rack of a pre-heated broiler and cook about 2 inches away from the heat source until the skins are well blistered and charred. Wrap the peppers in a clean towel and allow them to stand until cool. Peel off the skins with a small vegetable knife. Cut into thin strips and set aside. Place the chicken breasts between two sheets of plastic wrap and flatten by hitting with a rolling pin or meat mallet. Heat 1½ tbsps oil in a large

Heat the oil in a heavy frying pan or casserole and brown the venison on all sides over very high heat. Brown in several small batches if necessary. Remove the venison and lower the heat. If using a frying pan, transfer the venison to an ovenproof casserole. Lower the heat and brown the vegetables in the oil until golden. Sprinkle over the flour and cook until the flour browns lightly. Combine the vegetables with the venison and add the reserved marinade. Cover and cook the stew in a pre-heated 300°F oven for about 2 hours. Fifteen minutes before the end of cooking time, add the mushrooms and continue cooking until the meat is tender. Garnish with parsley before serving.

BRUNSWICK STEW

Peppers, potatoes, corn, tomatoes, onions and lima beans are staple ingredients in this recipe, which often includes squirrel in its really authentic version.

Preparation Time: 1 hour
Cooking Time: 2 hours
Serves: 6-8

INGREDIENTS

3lbs chicken portions
6 tbsps flour
3 tbsps butter or margarine

frying pan. Season the chicken breasts on both sides and place in the hot oil. Cook 5 minutes, turn over and cook until tender and lightly browned. Remove the chicken and keep it warm. Add the pepper strips, garlic, vinegar and green onions to the pan and cook briefly until the vinegar loses its strong aroma. Slice the chicken breasts across the grain into ¼ inch thick slices and arrange on serving plates. Spoon over the pan juices. Arrange the pepper mixture with the chicken and garnish with the sage leaves.

NEW ENGLAND ROAST TURKEY

The Thanksgiving celebration would not be the same without a turkey on the table. Native Indians first domesticated the bird and introduced the early settlers to it.

Preparation Time: 25-30 minutes
Cooking Time: 4-4½ hours
Serves: 10-12

INGREDIENTS

1 fresh turkey weighing about 20lbs
⅓ cup butter

SAUSAGE STUFFING

4 tbsps oil
4oz sausage meat
3 sticks celery, diced
2 onions, diced
1 cup chopped walnuts or pecans
1 cup raisins
1lb day-old bread, made into small cubes
1 cup chicken stock
¼ tsp each dried thyme and sage
2 tbsps chopped fresh parsley
Salt and pepper

METHOD

Singe any pin feathers on the turkey by holding the bird over a gas flame. Alternatively, pull out the feathers with tweezers. Remove the fat which is just inside the cavity of the bird. To prepare the stuffing, heat the oil and cook the sausage meat, breaking it up with a fork as it cooks. Add the celery, onion, nuts and raisins and cook for about 5 minutes, stirring constantly. Drain away the fat and add the herbs, cubes of bread and stock, and mix well. Season to taste. Stuff the cavity of the bird using your hands or a long-handled spoon. Save some stuffing to tuck under the neck flap to plump it. Sew the cavity of the bird closed, or use skewers to secure it. Tie the legs together but do not cross them over. Tuck the neck skin under the wing tips and, if desired, use a trussing needle and fine string to secure them. Place the turkey on a rack, breast side up, in a roasting pan. Soften the butter and spread some over the breast and the legs. Place the turkey in a pre-heated 325°F oven and cover loosely with foil. Roast for about 2 hours, basting often. Remove the foil and continue roasting for another 2-2½ hours, or until the internal temperature in the thickest part of the thigh registers 350°F. Alternatively, pierce the thigh with a skewer − if the juices run clear then the turkey is done. Allow to rest for about 15-20 minutes before carving. Make gravy with the pan juices if desired and serve.

CHICKEN POT PIE

Not a true pie, this dish is nevertheless warming winter fare with its creamy sauce and puffy biscuit topping.

Facing page: Mystic Seaport, Connecticut's recreated shipbuilding town, is a living monument to the state's seafaring past.

Left: Chicken Pot Pie.

Preparation Time: 25 minutes
Cooking Time: 20-30 minutes
Serves: 6

INGREDIENTS

4 chicken joints, 2 breasts and 2 legs
5 cups water
1 bay leaf
2 sprigs thyme
1 sprig rosemary
1 sprig fresh tarragon or ¼ tsp dry tarragon
4 whole peppercorns
1 allspice berry
4 tbsps white wine
2 carrots, peeled and diced
24 pearl onions, peeled
6 tbsps frozen corn kernels
½ cup heavy cream
Salt

BISCUIT TOPPING

3½ cups all-purpose flour
1½ tbsps baking powder
Pinch salt
5 tbsps butter or margarine
1½ cups milk
1 egg, beaten with a pinch of salt

METHOD

Place the chicken in a deep saucepan with water, herbs and spices and wine. Cover and bring to the boil. Reduce the heat and allow to simmer for 20-30 minutes, or until the chicken is tender. Remove the chicken from the pot and allow to cool. Skim and discard the fat from the surface of the stock. Skin the chicken and remove the meat from the bones. Continue to simmer the stock until reduced by about half. Strain the stock and add the carrots and onions. Cook until tender and add the corn. Stir in the cream and add the chicken. Pour into a casserole or into individual baking dishes. To prepare the topping, sift the dry ingredients into a bowl or place them in a food processor and process once or twice to sift. Rub in the butter or margarine until the mixture resembles small peas. Stir in enough of the milk until the mixture comes together. Turn out onto a floured surface and knead lightly. Roll out with a floured rolling pin and cut with a pastry cutter. Brush the surface of each biscuit with a mixture of egg and salt. Place the biscuits on top of the chicken mixture and bake for 10-15 minutes in a pre-heated oven at 375°F. Serve immediately.

Right: New Hampshire's abundant game is used to full effect in this attractive Brace of Duck in Pears and Grand Marnier presentation.

BRACE OF DUCK IN PEARS AND GRAND MARNIER

This dish is perfect for entertaining because it is impressive while being very easy to prepare. Fruit is always the perfect complement for the richness of duck and the mustard, Grand Marnier and honey add extra interest to the sauce. With New Hampshire's abundance of game, this sauce can also be used with wild duck.

Preparation Time: 20 minutes
Cooking Time: 50 minutes
Oven Temperature: 400°F
Serves: 4

INGREDIENTS

2 whole duck breasts cut from 6lb ducklings

SAUCE
2 ripe pears, peeled, cored and seeded
1 tsp mustard
1 cup Grand Marnier
1 cup honey

METHOD

Roast the two duck breasts in a hot oven for about 30 minutes. Meanwhile, prepare the sauce. Purée the pears with the mustard, Grand Marnier and honey. Simmer for about 20 minutes. When the duck has cooked for 30 minutes, drain off the fat, place the duck breasts back in the pan and pour over the sauce. Lower the oven temperature to 400°F and bake for another 20 minutes. Skim any fat from the sauce and pour over the duck to serve.

JAMES HALLER'S KITCHEN
PORTSMOUTH, NH

POACHED CHICKEN WITH CREAM SAUCE

Plainly cooked chicken can be as flavorful as it is attractive.

Preparation Time: 25 minutes
Cooking Time: 1 hour 10 minutes
Serves: 4

INGREDIENTS

4½lb whole roasting chicken
8-10 sticks celery, washed, cut into 3 inch lengths and tops reserved
4oz bacon, thickly sliced
2 cloves garlic, crushed
1 large onion, stuck with 4 cloves

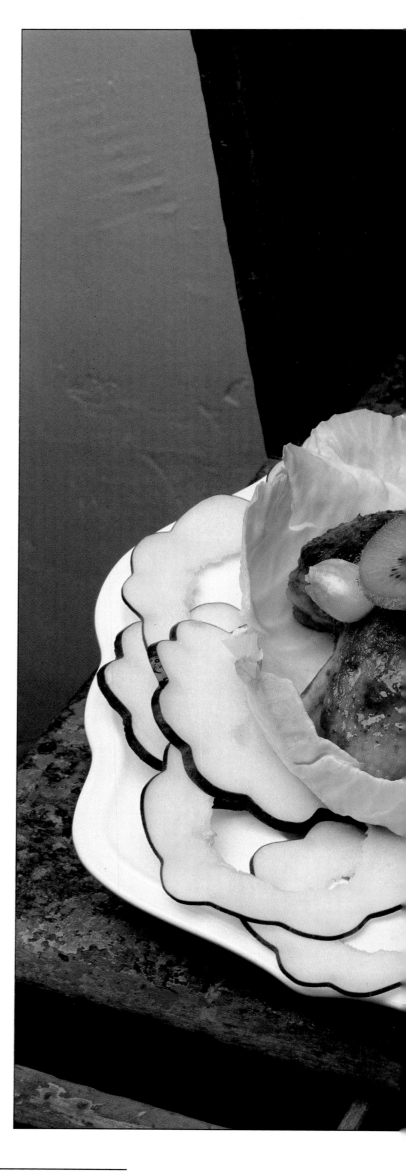

Facing page: Poached Chicken with Cream Sauce.

1 bay leaf
1 sprig fresh thyme
Salt and pepper
Water to cover
⅓ cup butter or margarine
6 tbsps flour
1 cup light cream

METHOD

Remove the fat from just inside the cavity of the chicken. Singe any pin feathers over gas flame or pull them out with tweezers. Tie the chicken legs together and tuck the wing tips under to hold the neck flap. Place the chicken in a large casserole or stock pot. Chop the celery tops and add to the pot. Place the bacon over the chicken and add the garlic, onion with the cloves, bay leaf, sprig thyme, salt, pepper and water to cover. Bring to the boil, reduce the heat and simmer gently, covered, for 50 minutes, or until the chicken is just tender. Cut the celery into 3 inch lengths and add to the chicken. Simmer a further 20 minutes, or until the celery is just tender. Remove the chicken to a serving plate and keep warm. Strain the stock and reserve the bacon and celery pieces. Skim fat off the top of the stock and add enough water to make up 2 cups, if necessary. Melt 1 tbsp of the butter or margarine in the casserole and sauté the bacon until just crisp. Drain on paper towels and crumble roughly. Melt the rest of the butter in the casserole or pan and when foaming take off the heat. Stir in the flour and gradually add the chicken stock. Add the cream and bring to the boil, stirring constantly. Simmer until the mixture is thickened. Untie the legs and trim the leg ends. If desired, remove the skin from the chicken and coat with the sauce. Garnish with the bacon and the reserved celery pieces.

Right: timeless farming methods in use by Pennsylvania's Amish community.

CHICKEN ST. PIERRE

A French name for a very Southern combination of chicken, lima beans, peppers and onions made into a spicy, aromatic stew.

Preparation Time: 35 minutes
Cooking Time: 40 minutes
Serves: 4-6

INGREDIENTS

3lb chicken, cut in 8 pieces
⅓ cup butter or margarine
3 tbsps flour
1 large red pepper, diced
1 large green pepper, diced
6 green onions, chopped
½ cup dry white wine
1 cup chicken stock
6oz lima beans
1 tsp chopped thyme
Salt, pepper and pinch nutmeg
Dash tabasco (optional)

METHOD

To cut the chicken in 8 pieces, remove the legs first. Cut between the legs and the body of the chicken. Bend the legs backwards to break the joint and cut away from the body. Cut the drumstick and thigh joints in half. Cut down the breastbone with a sharp knife and then use poultry shears to cut through the bone and ribcage to remove the breast joints from the back. Cut both breast joints in half, leaving some white meat attached to the wing joint. Cut through bones with poultry

shears. Heat the butter in a large sauté pan and when foaming add the chicken, skin side down. Brown on one side, turn over and brown other side. Remove the chicken and add the flour to the pan. Cook to a pale straw color. Add the peppers and onions and cook briefly. Pour on the wine and chicken stock and bring to the boil. Stir constantly until thickened. Add the chicken, lima beans, thyme, seasoning and nutmeg. Cover the pan and cook about 25 minutes, or until the chicken is tender. Add tabasco to taste, if desired, before serving.

COUNTRY CAPTAIN CHICKEN

A flavorful dish named for a sea captain with a taste for the spicy cuisine of India.

Preparation Time: 30 minutes
Cooking Time: 50 minutes
Serves: 6

INGREDIENTS

3lbs chicken portions
Seasoned flour
6 tbsps oil
1 medium onion, chopped
1 medium green pepper, seeded and chopped
1 clove garlic, crushed
Pinch salt and pepper
2 tsps curry powder
2 14oz cans tomatoes
2 tsps chopped parsley
1 tsp chopped marjoram
4 tbsps currants or raisins
4oz blanched almond halves

Above: Country Captain Chicken.
Left: the Alabama State Capitol, Montgomery.

METHOD

Remove skin from the chicken and dredge with flour, shaking off the excess. Heat the oil and brown the chicken on all sides until golden. Remove to an ovenproof casserole. Pour off all but 2 tbsps of the oil. Add the onion, pepper and garlic and cook slowly to soften. Add the seasonings and curry powder and cook, stirring frequently, for 2 minutes. Add the tomatoes, parsley, marjoram and bring to the boil. Pour the sauce over the chicken, cover and cook in a pre-heated 350°F oven for 45 minutes. Add the currants or raisins during the last 15 minutes. Meanwhile, toast the almonds in the oven on a baking sheet along with the chicken. Stir them frequently and watch carefully. Sprinkle over the chicken just before serving.

CORNISH HENS WITH SOUTHERN STUFFING

Cornbread makes a delicious stuffing and a change from the usual breadcrumb variations. Pecans, bourbon and ham give it a Southern flavor.

Preparation Time: 45-50 minutes
Cooking Time: 14 minutes cornbread
45 minutes–1 hour for the hens
Serves: 6

INGREDIENTS

Full quantity Corn Muffin recipe
2 tbsps butter or margarine
2 sticks celery, finely chopped
2 green onions, chopped
2oz chopped country or Smithfield ham
2oz chopped pecans
2 tbsps bourbon
Salt and pepper
1 egg, beaten
6 Cornish game hens
12 strips bacon

METHOD

Prepare the Corn Muffins according to the recipe, allow to cool completely and crumble finely. Melt the butter or margarine and soften the celery and onions for about 5 minutes over very low heat. Add the ham, pecans, cornbread crumbs and seasoning. Add bourbon and just enough egg to make a stuffing that holds together but is not too wet. Remove the giblets from the hens, if included, and fill each bird with stuffing. Sew up the cavity with fine string or close with small skewers. Criss-cross 2 strips of bacon over the breasts of each bird and tie or skewer the ends of the bacon together. Roast in a pre-heated 400°F oven for 45 minutes – 1 hour, or until tender. Baste the hens with the pan juices as they cook. Remove the bacon, if desired, during the last 15 minutes to brown the breasts, or serve with the bacon after removing the string or skewers.

Right: Cornish Hens with Southern Stuffing.

CHICKEN CROQUETTES

This is a delicious and economical way to use up leftover chicken. Try serving the croquettes with Mushroom Cream Sauce.

Preparation Time: 30 minutes
Cooking Time: 2-4 minutes each
Serves: 8-12

INGREDIENTS

2 cups dry bread crumbs
1½ cups chicken broth
4 cups cooked chicken
1 cup mushrooms
1 tsp chopped onion
½ cup chopped celery
½ tsp salt
⅛ tsp red pepper
1 tbsp chopped parsley
Dash lemon juice

TO FRY

1 cup dry bread crumbs
1 beaten egg
2 tbsps water or milk

METHOD

Soak the bread crumbs in the broth. Meanwhile, grind together the chicken and mushrooms, Combine with the soaked bread crumbs and the rest of the ingredients and allow to cool. Shape into 24 croquettes and chill. To cook, dip each croquette into dry bread crumbs, then into a mixture of beaten egg and water or milk, and finally into bread crumbs again. (This is the secret of good croquettes!) Fry in deep fat, heated to around 375°F, or until a 1 inch cube of bread browns in 1 minute, until golden (approximately 2-4 minutes).

COURTESY ELIZABETH C. KREMER
FROM THE TRUSTEES HOUSE DAILY
FARE, PLEASANT HILL, KENTUCKY
PLEASANT HILL PRESS, HARRODSBURG,
KENTUCKY 1970 AND 1977

Above: Chicken
Croquettes.

America Cooks

CHAPTER
5

VEGETABLES
AND SALADS

Previous pages: Butter Bean Salad – a salad with a difference from Alabama.
Facing page: Red Pepper Preserves can add color as well as spice to a main course or appetizer.

Below: Succotash, a dish with a particularly American history.

BUTTER BEAN SALAD

This salad is a delicious alternative to a mixed green salad, and could form the basis of a light luncheon when served with fresh, hot biscuits.

Preparation Time: 15 minutes
Cooking Time: 40 minutes
Serves: 8

INGREDIENTS

30oz fresh or frozen butter beans
4 cups water
1 tsp salt
4 hard-boiled eggs, chopped
1 small onion, finely grated
1 cup mayonnaise
¾ tsp prepared mustard
¾ tsp Worcestershire sauce
¾ tsp hot sauce

METHOD

Boil the butter beans in the water and salt for 40 minutes. Drain, then combine with the rest of the ingredients. Refrigerate the salad overnight and serve on a bed of lettuce.

STURDIVANT MUSEUM ASSOCIATION, SELMA, AL

RED PEPPER PRESERVES

This sweet but hot and spicy condiment adds a bright spot of color and Southwestern flavor to a main course or appetizer.

Preparation Time: 20 minutes
Cooking Time: 20-25 minutes
Makes: 2 cups

INGREDIENTS

5 red peppers, seeded
3 red or green chilies, seeded
1½ cups sugar
¾ cup red wine vinegar
1 cup liquid pectin

METHOD

Chop the peppers and chilies finely in a food processor. Combine the sugar and vinegar in a deep, heavy-based pan and heat gently to dissolve the sugar. Add the peppers and bring the mixture to the boil. Simmer for about 15 or 20 minutes. Stir in the pectin and return the mixture to the boil over high heat. Pour into sterilized jars and seal. Keep for up to one year in a cool, dark place.

SUCCOTASH

A tasty side dish with a strange name, this was inherited from the American Indians, who made it a full meal by adding meat or poultry to it.

Preparation Time: 10 minutes for frozen vegetables
25 minutes for fresh vegetables
Cooking Time: 5-8 minutes for frozen vegetables
8-10 minutes for fresh vegetables
Serves: 6

INGREDIENTS

4 oz fresh or frozen corn
4 oz fresh or frozen lima beans
4 oz fresh or frozen green beans
3 tbsps butter
Salt and pepper
Chopped parsley

METHOD

If using frozen vegetables, bring water to the boil in a saucepan and, when boiling, add the vegetables. Cook for about 5-8 minutes, drain and leave to dry. If using fresh vegetables, bring water to the boil in a saucepan and add the lima beans first. After about 2 minutes, add the green beans. Follow these with the corn about 3 minutes before the end of cooking time. Drain and leave to dry. Melt the butter in a saucepan and add the vegetables. Heat slowly, tossing or stirring occasionally, until heated through. Add salt and pepper to taste and stir in the parsley. Serve immediately.

CORN PUDDING

Preparation Time: 20 minutes
Cooking Time: 45 minutes
Oven Temperature: 350°F
Serves: 6-8

INGREDIENTS

2 cups Carnation milk or thin cream
2 cups canned or fresh corn
2 tbsps melted butter
2 tsps sugar
1 tsp salt
¼ tsp pepper
3 eggs, well beaten

METHOD

Add the milk, corn, butter, sugar and seasonings to the eggs. Pour into a well greased casserole and bake in a moderate oven for about 45 minutes or until the pudding is set. Insert a knife into the center of the pudding and if it comes out clean the pudding is done. For variety, add ¼ cup chopped green peppers or pimento, ½ cup minced ham or chopped mushrooms.

ISABELLA WITT,
DEAN'S MILL FARM,
STONINGTON, CT

Right: Grilled Vegetables, photographed at the home of Arnold Copper, Stonington.

GRILLED VEGETABLES

Cooking food outdoors has long been popular in the United States; it was in colonial times and still is to the present day. Vegetables are delicious with just a hint of charcoal taste and these can be used to accompany grilled meat or for a vegetarian barbecue.

Preparation Time: 30 minutes
Cooking Time: 15-20 minutes

INGREDIENTS

Any combination of the following: summer squash, zucchini squash, yellow onions, yellow, green or red peppers, scallions, large mushrooms, tomatoes, eggplant or other seasonal fresh vegetables

MARINADE
1 stick butter, melted
½ cup fresh lemon juice
Freshly ground pepper

METHOD

Prepare the vegetables as follows: cut summer squash and zucchini squash in half, lengthwise. Cut yellow onions in half around the equator and leave the peels on. Cut the peppers in half, lengthwise and remove the seeds but leave on the stems. Trim the root ends and the thin green ends of the scallions. Trim the stems from the mushrooms. Remove the stems from the tomatoes. Cut the eggplant in half, lengthwise or in quarters if very large. Melt the butter in a small saucepan and add the lemon juice and the pepper. Cook the onions, squashes and eggplant first as they will take the longest to cook. Baste the cut side of all the vegetables and place cut side down on the grill. When they have lightly browned, turn and baste well again. Complete the cooking of the squash, onions and eggplant on their skin sides. Halfway through their cooking time, add the peppers, mushrooms, scallions and tomatoes. Baste all the vegetables well as they cook. If using cherry tomatoes, warm them on the grill for a few seconds, but not for long or they will split and become mushy. The marinade is also excellent when used with chicken.

DANIEL ROUTHIER,
DEAN'S MILL FARM,
STONINGTON, CT

QUICK-FRIED VEGETABLES WITH HERBS

Crisply cooked vegetables with plenty of chives make a perfect side dish, hot or cold.

Preparation Time: 25 minutes
Cooking Time: 5 minutes
Serves: 6

INGREDIENTS

4 sticks celery
4 medium zucchini
2 red peppers, seeded
3-4 tbsps oil
Pinch salt and pepper
1 tsp chopped fresh oregano or marjoram
4 tbsps snipped fresh chives

METHOD

Slice the celery on the diagonal into pieces about 1½ inch thick. Cut the zucchini in half lengthwise and then cut into ½ inch thick slices. Remove all the seeds and the white pith from the peppers and cut them into diagonal pieces about 1 inch. Heat the oil in a heavy frying pan over medium high heat. Add the celery and stir-fry until barely tender. Add zucchini and peppers and stir-fry until all the vegetables are tender crisp. Add the salt, pepper and oregano or marjoram and cook for 30 seconds more. Stir in chives and serve immediately.

CRUDITÉ VEGETABLE PRESENTATION WITH NEW HAMPSHIRE HORSERADISH AND GARLIC DIP

Raw vegetables with dips are easy to prepare and serve and they add a splash of color to an hors d'oeuvre selection. Using a cabbage to hold the dip is a whimsical touch, and you can eat the dish!

Preparation Time: 40 minutes plus overnight chilling
Serves: 8-10

Facing page: the Scottish Rith Cathedral, Indianapolis.

Left: Quick-Fried Vegetables with Herbs.

INGREDIENTS

2 medium-size sweet potatoes
2 cups milk
2 eggs
¾ cup sugar
1 tsp cinnamon
¼ cup pecans, roughly chopped
2 tbsps butter
6 tbsps bourbon

METHOD

Peel the potatoes and grate them coarsely. Combine with the milk. Beat the eggs and gradually add the sugar, continuing until light and fluffy. Combine with the cinnamon and the pecans. Stir into the potatoes and milk and pour the mixture into a lightly buttered shallow baking dish. Dot with the remaining butter. Bake about 45 minutes to 1 hour in a pre-heated 350°F oven. Bake until the pudding is set and then pour over the bourbon just before serving.

TURNIP GREENS

Try these greens, which are familiar fare throughout the South.

Preparation Time: 15 minutes
Cooking Time: 45 minutes
Serves: 4

INGREDIENTS

2oz lean salt pork
2 cups boiling water
2lbs turnip greens
Salt to taste

METHOD

Rinse the salt pork, score several times and add to the boiling water. Simmer rapidly for 15 minutes. Meanwhile, wash the greens thoroughly and remove any tough stems. Tear into small pieces. Add to the pork, packing into the saucepan if necessary. Cover and simmer over medium heat for 30 minutes, or until the greens are tender. Taste the broth halfway through the cooking time and add salt if necessary.

CREATIVE CATERERS,
MONTGOMERY, AL

POTATO PANCAKE

This is a great favorite for lunch with apple sauce and is also good as a side dish with braised meats. The coarse grating blade of a food processor can be used to prepare the potatoes more quickly.

Preparation Time: 20-25 minutes
Cooking Time: 10-11 minutes
Serves: 6

INGREDIENTS

3lbs chef potatoes (not baking variety)
1 cup clarified butter
Salt and pepper

INGREDIENTS

½ lb broccoli flowerets, washed
¼ lb cauliflower flowerets, washed
¼ lb julienne strips of carrot and celery
4 asparagus tips, cut into 3-inch lengths
4 radish rosettes
8 sprigs fresh parsley
1 head red kale or Savoy cabbage

DIP

6oz fresh dairy sour cream
1 tbsp minced fresh garlic
1 tbsp minced fresh horseradish
½ tsp white pepper
½ tsp sea salt
¼ tsp dry mustard
1 tsp cognac

METHOD

Blend all the dip ingredients together and chill 24 hours. Make the radish rosettes and clean and trim the vegetables. Hollow out a space in the cabbage deep enough to hold the dip, fill and place in the middle of an attractive serving dish. Arrange all the vegetables around the cabbage to serve.

GREGORY MARTIN,
WHITE RABBIT CATERING,
HOOKSETT, NH

SWEET POTATO PUDDING

All puddings are not necessarily desserts. This one goes with meat or poultry for an unusual side dish.

Preparation Time: 25 minutes
Cooking Time: 45 minutes—1 hour
Serves: 6

Right: Boise, Idaho.

METHOD

Wash and peel the potatoes. Using a mandoline or grater, cut the potatoes into shoestring pieces. Place one or two tablespoons of the butter into a small skillet (5 inches in diameter) on medium heat. Put enough of the shoestring potatoes to cover the bottom of the pan into the hot butter. Season to taste with salt and pepper. Cook the potatoes over medium heat, shaking the pan frequently so they do not stick to the bottom. Press the potato mixture down into the pan with a spoon or spatula, lower the heat and continue cooking slowly for 5-6 minutes. Flip the pancake over and finish cooking the other side for an extra 5 minutes. Remove from the pan and serve immediately or keep warm. Repeat the process until all the potato is used.

NEW ENGLAND CULINARY INSTITUTE,
MONTPELIER, VT

ALL-AMERICAN POTATO SALAD

Here is a delicious salad to serve with the Triple Bean Salad Piquant for a gorgeous summer meal.

Preparation Time: 15 minutes
Cooking Time: 2 hours or more
Serves: 8

INGREDIENTS

4 cups diced cold boiled potatoes
1-2 tbsps minced onion
¼ cup celery, chopped (optional)
2 tbsps chopped pimento
½ cup mayonnaise
¼ cup chopped dill pickle
½ tsp prepared mustard
½ tsp salt
Pepper to taste
2-3 hard-boiled eggs, coarsely chopped

METHOD

Combine all the ingredients except for the eggs, and toss carefully until well mixed. Add the eggs, reserving some for a garnish, and mix gently. Garnish the salad with the reserved eggs and chill for at least 2 hours before serving.

DORIS BELCHER, MEMPHIS, TN

CREAMED ONIONS

Whole small onions in a creamy, rich sauce are part of Thanksgiving fare, but they are too good to save for just once a year.

Preparation Time: 30 minutes
Cooking Time: 10 minutes for the onions and 10 minutes for the sauce
Serves: 4

INGREDIENTS

1lb pearl onions
Boiling water to cover
2 cups milk
1 bay leaf
1 blade mace

Facing page: Squash
with Blueberries.

2 tbsps butter or margarine
2 tbsps flour
Pinch salt and white pepper
Chopped parsley (optional)

METHOD

Trim the root hairs on the onions but do not cut the roots off completely. Place the onions in a large saucepan and pour over the boiling water. Bring the onions back to the boil and cook for about 10 minutes. Transfer the onions to cold water, allow to cool completely and then peel off the skins, removing roots as well. Leave the onions to drain dry. Place the milk in a deep saucepan and add the blade mace and the bay leaf. Bring just to the boil, take off the heat and allow to stand for 15 minutes. Melt the butter in a large saucepan and, when foaming, stir in the flour. Strain on the milk and discard the bay leaf and blade mace. Stir well and bring to the boil. Allow the sauce to simmer for about 3 minutes to thicken. Add salt and white pepper to taste and stir in the onions. Cook to heat through, but do not allow the sauce to boil again. Serve immediately and garnish with chopped parsley, if desired.

STUFFED ACORN SQUASH WITH A RUM GLAZE

Squash has a subtle flavor that blends well with other ingredients.

Preparation Time: 30 minutes
Cooking Time: 1 hour
Serves: 4

INGREDIENTS

2 even-sized acorn squash
⅓ cup butter or margarine

Right: Stuffed Acorn
Squash with a Rum
Glaze.

2 cooking apples, peeled, cored and cut into
½ inch pieces
½ cup pitted prunes, cut into large pieces
1 cup dried apricots, cut into large pieces
½ tsp ground allspice
6 tbsps rum
½ cup chopped walnuts
½ cup golden raisins
½ cup packed light brown sugar

METHOD

Cut the squash in half lengthwise. Scoop out and discard the seeds. Place the squash skin side up in a baking dish with water to come halfway up the sides. Bake for about 30 minutes at 350°F. Melt half the butter in a saucepan and add the apple, prunes and apricots. Add the allspice and rum and bring to the boil. Lower the heat and simmer gently for about 5-10 minutes. Add the nuts and golden raisins 3 minutes before the end of cooking time. Turn the squash over and fill the hollow with the fruit. Reserve the fruit cooking liquid. Melt the remaining butter in a saucepan and stir in the brown sugar. Melt slowly until the sugar forms a syrup. Pour on fruit cooking liquid, stirring constantly. Bring back to the boil and cook until syrupy. Add more water if necessary. Spoon the glaze onto each squash, over the fruit and the cut edge. Bake for a further 30 minutes, or until the squash is tender.

SQUASH WITH CALIFORNIA BLUEBERRIES

This vegetable dish will steal the scene at any meal, so serve it with simply cooked poultry or meat.

Preparation Time: 30 minutes
Cooking Time: 50-55 minutes
Serves: 6

INGREDIENTS

2 acorn squash
1 small apple, peeled and chopped
4 tbsps light brown sugar
Freshly grated nutmeg
4 tbsps butter or margarine
6oz fresh or frozen blueberries

METHOD

Cut the squash in half lengthwise. Scoop out the seeds and discard them. Fill the hollows with the chopped apple. Sprinkle on the sugar and nutmeg and dot with the butter or margarine. Place the squash in a baking dish and pour in about 1″ of water. Bake, covered, for 40-45 minutes at 375°F. Uncover, add the blueberries and cook an additional 10 minutes.

HARVARD BEETS

One of the best known dishes using this readily available root vegetable. The color makes this a perfect accompaniment to plain meat or poultry.

Preparation Time: 20 minutes
Cooking Time: 40-50 minutes
Serves: 6

Left: Sunset over Upper
Herring Lake, Michigan.

INGREDIENTS

2lbs small beets
Boiling water
3 tbsps cornstarch
½ cup sugar
Pinch salt and pepper
1 cup white wine vinegar
¾ cup reserved beet cooking liquid
2 tbsps butter

METHOD

Choose even-sized beets and cut off the tops, if necessary. Place beets in a large saucepan of water. Cover the pan and bring to the boil. Lower the heat and cook gently until tender, about 30-40 minutes. Add more boiling water as necessary during cooking. Drain the beets, reserving the liquid, and allow the beets to cool. When the beets are cool, peel them and slice into ¼ inch rounds, or cut into small dice. Combine the cornstarch, sugar, salt and pepper, vinegar and required amount of beet liquid in a large saucepan. Bring to the boil over moderate heat, stirring constantly until thickened. Return the beets to the saucepan and allow to heat through for about 5 minutes. Stir in the butter and serve immediately.

NAPA VALLEY ARTICHOKES

The Napa Valley is wine growing country, so white wine is a natural choice for cooking one of California's best-loved vegetables.

Preparation Time: 30 minutes
Cooking Time: 40 minutes
Serves: 4

Above: Napa Valley
Artichokes.

Facing page: Zucchini Slippers.

INGREDIENTS

4 globe artichokes
4 tbsps olive oil
1 clove garlic, left whole
1 small bay leaf
1 sprig fresh rosemary
2 parsley stalks
4 black peppercorns
2 lemon slices
1 cup dry white wine
1 tbsp chopped parsley
Pinch salt and pepper
Lemon slices to garnish

METHOD

Trim stems on the base of the artichokes so that they sit upright. Peel off any damaged bottom leaves. Trim the spiny tips off all the leaves with scissors. Trim the top 1″ off the artichokes with a sharp knife. Place the artichokes in a large, deep pan with all the ingredients except the parsley. Cover the pan and cook about 40 minutes, or until artichokes are tender and bottom leaves pull away easily. Drain upside down on paper towels. Boil the cooking liquid to reduce slightly. Strain, add parsley and serve with the artichokes. Garnish with lemon slices.

CABBAGE AND PEANUT SLAW

Boiled dressings are old favorites in the South. This one gives a lively sweet-sour taste to basic coleslaw.

Preparation Time: 30 minutes
Serves: 6

Right: Cabbage and Peanut Slaw.

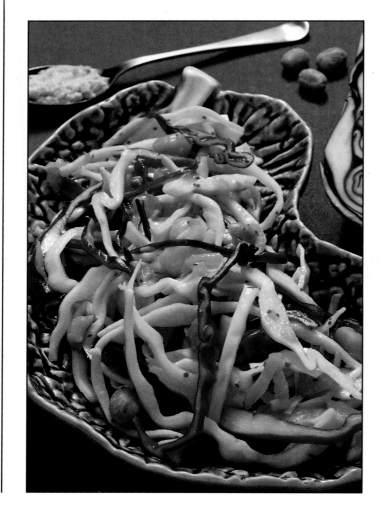

INGREDIENTS

1 small head white cabbage, finely shredded
2 carrots, shredded
2 tsps celery seed
1 cup dry-roasted peanuts
1 egg
½ cup white wine vinegar
½ cup water
½ tsp dry mustard
2 tbsps sugar

METHOD

Combine the vegetables, celery seed and peanuts in a large bowl. Beat the egg in a small bowl. Add vinegar, water, mustard and sugar and blend thoroughly. Place the bowl in a pan of very hot water and whisk until thickened. Cool and pour over the vegetables.

ZUCCHINI SLIPPERS

Preparation Time: 30 minutes
Cooking Time: 23-25 minutes
Serves: 6

INGREDIENTS

6 even-sized zucchini
4oz cottage cheese, drained
4oz grated Colby cheese
1 small red pepper, seeded and chopped
2 tbsps chopped parsley
Pinch salt and cayenne pepper
1 large egg
Watercress or parsley to garnish

METHOD

Trim the ends of the zucchini and cook in boiling salted water for about 8 minutes, or steam for 10 minutes. Remove from the water or steamer and cut in half. Allow to cool slightly and then scoop out the center, leaving a narrow margin of flesh on the skin to form a shell. Invert each zucchini slipper onto a paper towel to drain, reserving the scooped-out flesh. Chop the flesh and mix with the remaining ingredients. Spoon filling into the shells and arrange in a greased baking dish. Bake, uncovered, in a pre-heated 350°F oven for 15 minutes. Broil, if desired, to brown the top. Garnish with watercress or parsley.

CORN IN THE SHUCK

Southern cooks have developed special methods to preserve the wonderful fresh flavor of summer vegetables. Here is an example.

METHOD

Cut off the top 2 inches of an ear of corn to remove the silk. Remove the outer leaves of the shuck down to the fresh green leaves. Boil the ears in a covered pot for one hour. Remove from the water and pull back the shuck enough to wrap a napkin around it and use it as a handle. Dip the corn in melted butter, then salt and pepper to taste. Corn cooked in this way will retain all of its delicious natural flavor.

BENNETT A BROWN III,
LOWCOUNTRY BARBEQUE CATERING,
ATLANTA, GA

Above: Fresh Creamed Mushrooms.

FRESH CREAMED MUSHROOMS

For a recipe that has been around since Colonial times, this one is surprisingly up-to-date.

Preparation Time: 20 minutes
Cooking Time: 7 minutes
Serves: 4

INGREDIENTS

1lb even-sized button mushrooms
1 tbsp lemon juice
2 tbsps butter or margarine
1 tbsp flour
Salt and white pepper
¼ tsp freshly grated nutmeg
1 small bay leaf
1 blade mace
1 cup heavy cream
1 tbsp dry sherry

METHOD

Wash the mushrooms quickly and dry them well. Trim the stems level with the caps. Leave whole if small, halve or quarter if large. Toss with the lemon juice and set aside. In a medium saucepan, melt the butter or margarine and stir in the flour. Cook, stirring gently, for about 1 minute. Remove from the heat, add the nutmeg, salt, pepper, bay leaf and mace and gradually stir in the cream. Return the pan to the heat and bring to the boil, stirring constantly. Allow to boil for about 1 minute, or until thickened. Reduce the heat and add the mushrooms. Simmer gently, covered, for about 5 minutes, or until the mushrooms are tender. Add the sherry during the last few minutes of cooking. Remove bay leaf and blade mace. Sprinkle with additional grated nutmeg before serving.

Right: opulent Southern architecture on Jekyll Island, off the coast of Georgia, recalls a bygone age.

HOT PEPPER RELISH

Prepare this colorful relish in the summer, when peppers are plentiful, but save some to brighten up winter meals, too.

Preparation Time: 30 minutes
Cooking Time: 45 minutes
Makes: 4 cups

INGREDIENTS

*3lbs sweet peppers (even numbers of red, green,
yellow and orange, or as available), seeded
4-6 red or green chilies, seeded and finely chopped
2 medium onions, finely chopped
½ tsp oregano
½ tsp ground coriander
2 bay leaves
Salt to taste
2 cups granulated or preserving sugar
1½ cups white wine vinegar or white distilled vinegar*

METHOD

Cut the peppers into small dice and combine with the chilies and onions in a large saucepan. Pour over boiling water to cover, and return to the boil. Cook rapidly for 10 minutes and drain well. Meanwhile, combine the sugar and vinegar in a large saucepan. Bring slowly to the boil to dissolve the sugar, stirring occasionally. When the peppers and onions have drained, add them and the remaining ingredients to the vinegar and sugar. Bring back to the boil and then simmer for 30 minutes. Remove the bay leaves and pour into sterilized jars and seal.

BAKED VIDALIA ONIONS

Vidalia onions are large, sweet onions which are flat at both ends. They are grown in the area surrounding Vidalia, Georgia and are delicious eaten raw.

METHOD

To prepare, peel off the outer skin of the onion and cut a thin slice off both ends so that the onion will sit flat. Cut a small well into one end. Place a bouillon cube inside and cover with a pat of butter. Wrap the onion with a square of heavy aluminum foil. Place the wrapped onions on a baking sheet and bake at 350°F for 1½-2 hours, or until the onion is soft. Loosen the foil and transfer the onion to a small bowl using a slotted spoon. Pour the juices over the onion to serve.

ANN DORSEY, FULL SERVICE CATERING,
ATLANTA, GA

COLESLAW

The unusual salad dressing, delicately flavored with dill, makes this coleslaw something special.

Preparation Time: 30 minutes
Serves: 6-8

INGREDIENTS

*1 medium cabbage, shredded
3 carrots, shredded*

Above: Baked Vidalia Onions.

Facing page: Hot Pepper Relish.

Above: Boston Baked Beans, the original American "fast food."

METHOD

Combine the cucumber and onion slices. Sprinkle with the salt and sugar, then add the vinegar and celery seed. Mix thoroughly to combine. Cover and chill until ready to serve.

Garnish this crisp, cool salad with slivers of red radishes for a lovely summery contrast.

PAT COKER, NASHVILLE, TN

BOSTON BAKED BEANS

The first American "fast food", these beans were frozen and taken on long journeys to re-heat and eat en route.

Preparation Time: 20 minutes with overnight soaking
for the beans
Cooking Time: 3½ hours
Serves: 6-8

INGREDIENTS

1lb dried navy beans
5 cups water
4oz salt pork or slab bacon
1 onion, peeled and left whole
1 tsp dry mustard
⅓-½ cup molasses
Salt and pepper

METHOD

Soak the beans overnight in the water. Transfer to fresh water to cover. Bring to the boil and allow to cook for about 10 minutes. Drain and reserve the liquid. Place the beans, salt pork or bacon and whole onion in a large, deep casserole or bean pot. Mix the molasses, mustard, salt and pepper with 1 cup of the reserved bean liquid. Stir into the beans and add enough bean liquid to cover. Expose only the pork rind on the salt pork and cover the casserole. Bake in a pre-heated 300°F oven for about 2 hours. Add the remaining liquid, stirring well, and cook a further 1½ hours, or until the beans are tender. Uncover the beans for the last 30 minutes. To serve, remove and discard the onion. Take out the salt pork or bacon and remove the rind. Slice or dice the meat and return to the beans. Check the seasoning and serve.

DRESSING

¾ cup mayonnaise
loz red wine vinegar
½ tbsp dill
¼ tsp salt
⅛ tsp pepper

METHOD

Combine the shredded carrots and cabbage in a large bowl. To prepare the dressing, blend all the dressing ingredients together in a separate bowl until smooth. Pour this dressing over the shredded vegetables and toss until well coated. Chill well before serving.

ANN DORSEY, FULL SERVICE CATERING,
ATLANTA, GA

MARINATED CUCUMBERS

Preparation Time: 20 minutes
Serves: 8

INGREDIENTS

4 cucumbers, sliced
1 small onion, thinly sliced
¼ cup sugar
⅔ cup vinegar
½ tsp celery seed
1½ tsps salt

Facing page: Scotts Bluff, Nebraska.

SOUTHERN-STYLE POTATO SOUP

Makes a refreshing soup on a hot day.

Preparation Time: 30 minutes, plus chilling
Cooking Time: approximately 50 minutes
Yield: 1½ quarts

INGREDIENTS

1½ cups green onions, white part only, diced
½ cup onions, chopped
1 tbsp butter
3 cups baking potatoes, peeled and diced
3 cups hot water
3 tsps salt
1 cup hot milk
½ tsp white pepper
1 cup light cream
1 cup heavy cream
8 tsps chopped chives

METHOD

In a heavy 4-quart pot, sauté the onions in the butter until soft, but not brown. Add the potatoes, hot water and 2 tsps of the salt. Simmer, uncovered, for 30-40 minutes, or until the potatoes are soft. Liquidize the potatoes and onions, and return to the pot. Add the hot milk, and slowly bring the soup to a boil, stirring often to keep the potatoes from settling. Add the remaining salt and the pepper. Remove from the heat and strain through a sieve. Cool the soup, stir, then strain again and add the light and heavy cream. Serve chilled and garnished with the chopped chives.

STURDIVANT MUSEUM ASSOCIATION,
SELMA, AL

Far left: the dramatic Chicago nighttime skyline. The city's rich ethnic mix ensures a widely varied choice of culinary styles.

Left: Walnut Grove Salad.

WALNUT GROVE SALAD

Walnut Grove is a town famous for its walnuts! They add their crunch to a colorful variation on coleslaw.

Preparation Time: 25-30 minutes
Serves: 6

INGREDIENTS

1 small head red cabbage
1 avocado, peeled and cubed
1 carrot, grated
4 green onions, shredded
1 cup chopped walnuts
6 tbsps oil
2 tbsps white wine vinegar
2 tsps dry mustard
Salt and pepper

METHOD

Cut the cabbage in quarters and remove the core. Use a large knife to shred finely or use the thick slicing blade on a food processor. Prepare the avocado as for Avocado Soup and cut it into small cubes. Combine the cabbage, avocado and shredded carrot with the onions and walnuts in a large bowl. Mix the remaining ingredients together well and pour over the salad. Toss carefully to avoid breaking up the avocado. Chill before serving.

HEARTY SPINACH SALAD

This salad is substantial enough to be served as a light luncheon dish.

Preparation Time: 15 minutes
Serves: 6

INGREDIENTS

1lb spinach
½lb fresh mushrooms, sliced
3 hard-boiled eggs, sliced
6 slices bacon, cooked and crumbled

METHOD

Wash the spinach thoroughly and tear it into bite-sized pieces. Toss the spinach with the mushrooms, eggs and bacon in a large salad bowl. Pour Green Goddess Salad Dressing over and serve at once.

ANN HALL, GREY OAKS,
VICKSBURG, MS

CHARTREUSE OF VEGETABLES

A chartreuse in French cooking is a molded dish that has one main ingredient complemented by smaller quantities of choicer ingredients, in this case, fluffy mashed potatoes with a selection of colorful garden vegetables. Be generous with the quantity of mashed potatoes because this is what holds the dish together. Don't be afraid to try it; it only *looks* complicated.

Preparation Time: 40 minutes
Cooking Time: 25 minutes
Oven Temperature: 425°F
Serves: 6-8

INGREDIENTS

Potatoes, peeled and cubed
Carrots, cut in julienne strips
String beans, trimmed
Peas
Zucchini
Summer squash
Cabbage leaves
Brussels sprouts
Cauliflower flowerets

METHOD

Cook the potatoes about 20 minutes and drain them well. Dry over heat while mashing. Trim the carrot sticks and string beans to fit the height of a soufflé dish. Slice the zucchini and summer squash, trim down thick ribs of the cabbage leaves and trim the ends of the Brussels sprouts. Parboil all the vegetables for about 2 minutes. Drain and rinse under cold water and leave to dry. Butter a soufflé dish thickly. Arrange a row of peas along the edge of the bottom of the dish. Next to the peas arrange a row of sliced zucchini and

then fill in the center with circles of summer squash. Line the sides of the dish with carrot sticks and string beans, alternating the two. Butter will hold the vegetables in place. Carefully spread a layer of mashed potato over the bottom and up the sides to completely cover the carrots and beans. Add a thick layer to hold the vegetables together. Place a cabbage leaf or two on top of the potatoes and press gently to firm the vegetables. On the cabbage make a circle of Brussels sprouts around the outside edge and fill in the center with cauliflower. On top of that arrange another circle of zucchini and summer squash. Top with a cabbage leaf and fill with more mashed potatoes, smoothing the top. Bake in a preheated 425°F oven for 20 minutes. Remove from the oven and allow to set for 3-5 minutes before inverting onto a serving dish. If necessary, loosen the sides of the chartreuse from the dish with a sharp knife before turning out.

JAMES HALLER'S KITCHEN
SOUTH BERWICK, ME

MINTED MIXED VEGETABLES

Carrots, cucumber and zucchini are all complemented by the taste of fresh mint. In fact, most vegetables are, so experiment.

Preparation Time: 25-30 minutes
Cooking Time: 6-10 minutes
Serves: 4-6

INGREDIENTS

3 medium carrots
1 cucumber
2 zucchini
½ cup water
1 tsp sugar
Pinch salt
1½ tbsps butter, cut into small pieces
1 tbsp coarsely chopped fresh mint leaves

METHOD

Peel the carrots and cut them into sticks about ½ inch thick and 2½ inches long. Peel the cucumber and cut it into quarters. Remove the centers and cut into sticks the same size as the carrots. Cut the zucchini into sticks the same size as the other vegetables. Combine the carrots, water, sugar and salt in a medium saucepan. Cover the pan and bring to the boil over high heat. Reduce the heat to medium and cook for about 3 minutes. Uncover the pan and cook a further 3 minutes. Increase the heat and add the cucumber and zucchini and boil until the vegetables are tender crisp. Add the butter and stir over heat until melted and the liquid has completely evaporated, glazing the vegetables. Remove from the heat, add the mint and toss well.

PARKE'S SALAMAGUNDI

This attractive salad is an early summer favorite in Virginia.

Preparation Time: 30 minutes
Serves: 6-8

INGREDIENTS

1lb Virginia ham, julienned
1lb chicken or turkey, julienned
6 hard-boiled eggs, sliced
8oz anchovy fillets
4oz sardines in olive oil
Assorted pickles
Celery hearts
Assorted salad greens
1 cup or more of your favorite French dressing

METHOD

Arrange the meat and fish in a circular pattern on a large serving platter. Surround with the celery hearts, salad greens and pickles. Pour a light coating of French dressing over all just before serving.

WOODLAWN PLANTATION COOK BOOK,
JOAN SMITH, EDITOR,
MOUNT VERNON, VA

CREOLE TOMATOES

A perfect side dish for grilled chicken or fish, this is especially good for summer, when tomatoes are at their best.

Preparation Time: 30 minutes
Cooking Time: 15-20 minutes
Serves: 4

INGREDIENTS

4 large ripe tomatoes
1 small green pepper, seeded and thinly sliced
4 green onions, sliced
1 clove garlic, crushed
4 tbsps white wine
Pinch cayenne pepper
Salt
1 tbsp butter or margarine
4 tbsps heavy cream

METHOD

Remove the tomato stems and place tomatoes in a pan of boiling water. Leave for 30 seconds and remove with a

Left: Parke's Salamagundi, a summer favorite in Virginia.

Above: Creole Tomatoes from Louisiana are a perfect side dish for grilled chicken or fish.

draining spoon. Place immediately in a bowl of ice cold water. Use a small, sharp knife to remove the peel, beginning at the stem end. Cut the tomatoes in half and scoop out the seeds. Strain the juice and reserve it, discarding the seeds. Place tomatoes cut side down in a baking dish and sprinkle over the reserved juice. Add the sliced pepper, onions, garlic, wine, cayenne pepper and salt. Dot with butter or margarine. Place in a preheated 350°F oven for about 15-20 minutes, or until tomatoes are heated through and tender, but not falling apart. Strain juices into a small saucepan. Bring juices to the boil to reduce slightly. Stir in the cream and reboil. Spoon over the tomatoes to serve.

SQUASH SIDE DISH

Preparation Time: 20 minutes
Cooking Time: 15 minutes
Serves: 8

INGREDIENTS

3 tbsps butter

Facing page: Squash Side Dish.

1 medium onion, chopped
1 medium bell pepper, diced
2 medium zucchini squash, sliced
2 medium yellow summer squash, sliced
14½oz can tomato wedges
½ tsp garlic salt
Salt and pepper to taste

GARNISH

Fresh parsley
Grated Parmesan cheese

METHOD

Melt the butter in a heavy skillet, add the onion and cook until transparent. Stir in the bell pepper and continue cooking until soft. Add the squash and seasonings, cover, and simmer until just tender. Drain the tomatoes, reserving the liquid, and add them to the skillet. Cook for an additional 5 to 8 minutes, adding some of the reserved liquid if needed.

Garnish this colorful dish with parsley and sprinkle with Parmesan cheese before serving.

DORIS BELCHER, MEMPHIS, TN

FRIED OKRA

Cornmeal and okra, two Southern specialties, combine in a classic vegetable dish that's delicious with meat, poultry, game or fish.

Preparation Time: 15-20 minutes
Cooking Time: 3 minutes per batch
Serves: 4-6

INGREDIENTS

1 cup yellow cornmeal
1 tsp salt
2 eggs, beaten
1½lbs fresh okra, washed, stemmed and cut crosswise
into ½ inch thick slices
2 cups oil for frying

Left: fertile farmland in Crawford County, Iowa.

METHOD

Combine the cornmeal and salt on a plate. Coat okra pieces in the beaten egg. Dredge the okra in the mixture. Place the oil in a large, deep sauté pan and place over moderate heat. When the temperature reaches 375°F add the okra in batches and fry until golden brown. Drain thoroughly on paper towels and serve immediately.

Above: Fried Okra. Brought to America by African Slaves, okra is a popular vegetable in Southern cooking.

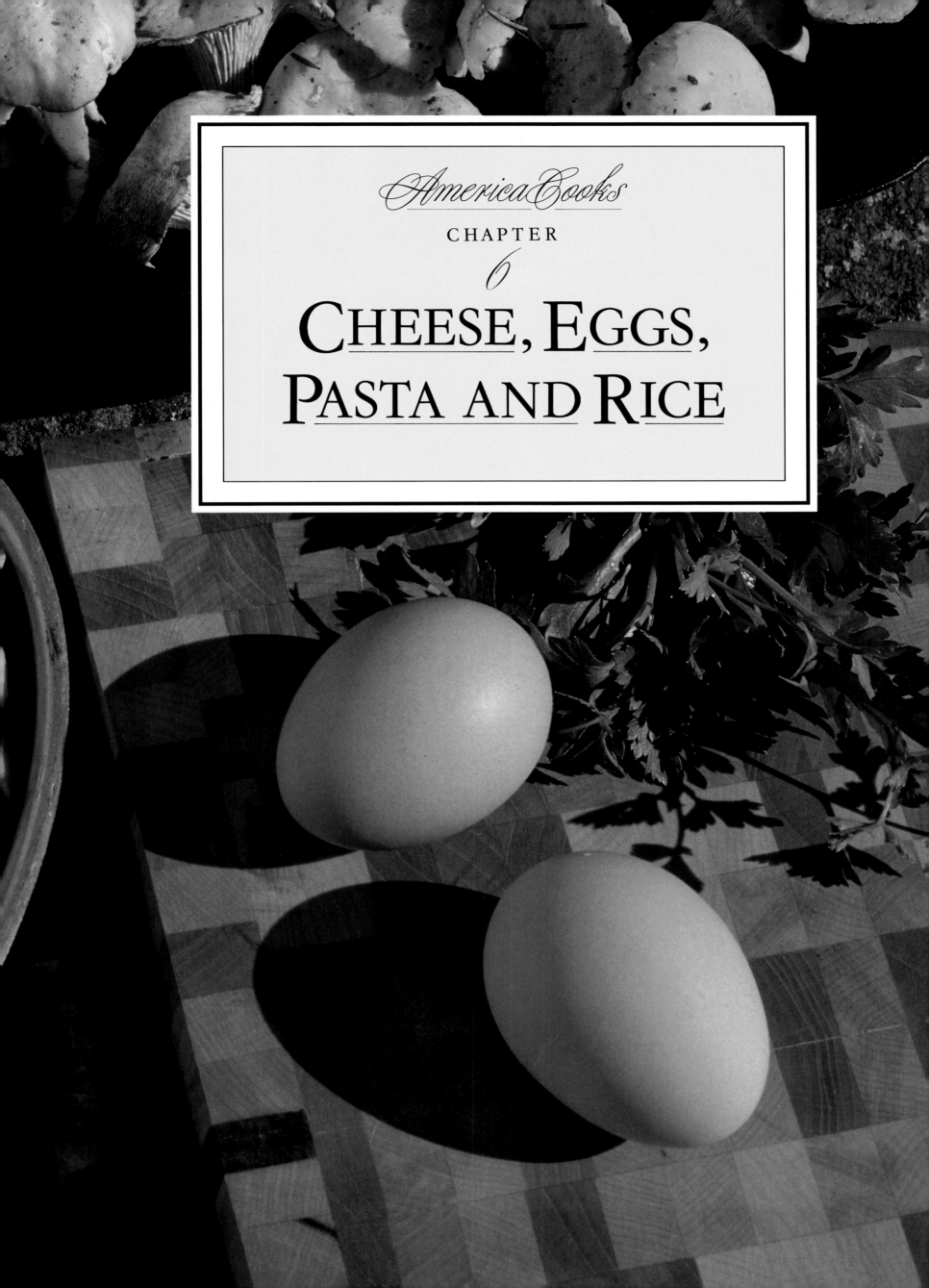

America Cooks

CHAPTER

6

CHEESE, EGGS, PASTA AND RICE

CHANTERELLE OMELET

Chanterelles, those very French mushrooms, are also frequently found growing wild in wooded areas in Vermont. Avoid washing them, since they absorb water. Just wipe them with damp paper towels if cleaning is necessary. The omelet itself takes less than a minute to cook, so all the ingredients should be at hand before proceeding.

Preparation Time: 15 minutes
Cooking Time: 2-3 minutes
Serves: 1

INGREDIENTS

2 tbsps butter
3 eggs at room temperature
3oz fresh chanterelle mushrooms
2 tbsps finely chopped parsley
Salt and pepper

METHOD

Slice the mushrooms and melt 1 tbsp of the butter in a small pan. Sauté the mushrooms quickly, season with salt and pepper and add the chopped parsley. Set aside and keep them warm. Beat the eggs thoroughly with a fork or whisk in a small bowl. Place the remaining butter in an omelet pan and heat until foaming but not brown. Pour in the eggs and swirl over the bottom of the pan. Immediately stir the eggs with a fork to allow the uncooked mixture to fall to the bottom of the pan. When the mixture is creamily set on top, scatter over the sautéed chanterelles and roll the omelet in the pan by flipping about a third of it to the middle and then flipping it out onto a hot plate.

NEW ENGLAND CULINARY INSTITUTE,
MONTPELIER, VT

SAN FRANCISCO RICE

This rice and pasta dish has been popular for a long time in San Francisco, where it was invented.

Preparation Time: 25 minutes
Cooking Time: 20 minutes
Serves: 4

Above left: California
Wild Rice Pilaff.
Above: Spicy Rice and
Beans.

INGREDIENTS

4oz uncooked long grain rice
4oz uncooked spaghetti, broken into 2" pieces
3 tbsps oil
4 tbsps sesame seeds
2 tbsps chopped chives
Salt and pepper
1½ cups chicken, beef or vegetable stock
1 tbsp soy sauce
2 tbsps chopped parsley

METHOD

Rinse the rice and pasta to remove starch, and leave to drain dry. Heat the oil in a large frying pan and add the dried rice and pasta. Cook over moderate heat to brown the rice and pasta, stirring continuously. Add the sesame seeds and cook until the rice, pasta and seeds are golden brown. Add the chives, salt and pepper, and pour over 1 cup stock. Stir in the soy sauce and bring to the boil. Cover and cook about 20 minutes, or until the rice and pasta are tender and the stock is absorbed. Add more of the reserved stock as necessary. Do not let the rice and pasta dry out during cooking. Fluff up the grains of rice with a fork and sprinkle with the parsley before serving.

CALIFORNIA WILD RICE PILAFF

Wild rice adds a nutty taste and a texture contrast to rice pilaff. It's good as a side dish or stuffing.

Preparation Time: 25 minutes
Cooking Time: 20 minutes
Serves: 4

INGREDIENTS

4oz uncooked long-grain rice, rinsed
2oz wild rice, rinsed
1 tbsp oil
1 tbsp butter or margarine
2 sticks celery, finely chopped
2 green onions
4 tbsps chopped walnuts or pecans
4 tbsps raisins
1½ cups chicken or vegetable stock

METHOD

Heat the oil in a frying pan and drop in the butter. When foaming, add both types of rice. Cook until the white rice looks clear. Add celery and chop the green onions, reserving the dark green tops to use as a garnish. Add the white part of the onions to the rice and celery and cook briefly to soften. Add the walnuts or pecans, raisins and stock. Bring to the boil, cover and cook until the rice absorbs the liquid and is tender. Sprinkle with reserved chopped onion tops.

SPICY RICE AND BEANS

A lively side dish or vegetarian main course, this recipe readily takes to creative variations and even makes a good cold salad.

Preparation Time: 25 minutes
Cooking Time: 50 minutes
Serves: 6-8

INGREDIENTS

4 tbsps oil
2 cups long grain rice
1 onion, finely chopped

1 green pepper, seeded and chopped
1 tsp each ground cumin and coriander
1-2 tsps tabasco sauce
Salt
3½ cups stock
1lb canned red kidney beans, drained and rinsed
1lb canned tomatoes, drained and coarsely chopped
Chopped parsley

METHOD

Heat the oil in a casserole or a large, deep saucepan. Add the rice and cook until just turning opaque. Add the onion, pepper and cumin and coriander. Cook gently for a further 2 minutes. Add the tabasco, salt, stock and beans and bring to the boil. Cover and cook about 45 minutes, or until the rice is tender and most of the liquid is absorbed. Remove from the heat and add the tomatoes, stirring them in gently. Leave to stand, covered, for 5 minutes. Fluff up the mixture with a fork and sprinkle with parsley to serve.

CHILI RELLENOS

Organization is the key to preparing these stuffed peppers. Fried inside their golden batter coating, they're puffy and light.

Preparation Time: 40 minutes
Cooking Time: 3 minutes per pepper
sauce 15 minutes
Serves: 8

INGREDIENTS

Full quantity Red Sauce
(see recipe for Southwestern Stir- fry)
8 small green peppers
4 small green chilies, seeded and finely chopped
1 clove garlic, crushed
1 tsp chopped fresh sage
8oz cream cheese

Far right: the Mission of San Miguel in Santa Fe. Sometimes fiery and often colorful, recipes from this region are always popular. Above right: Chili Rellenos.

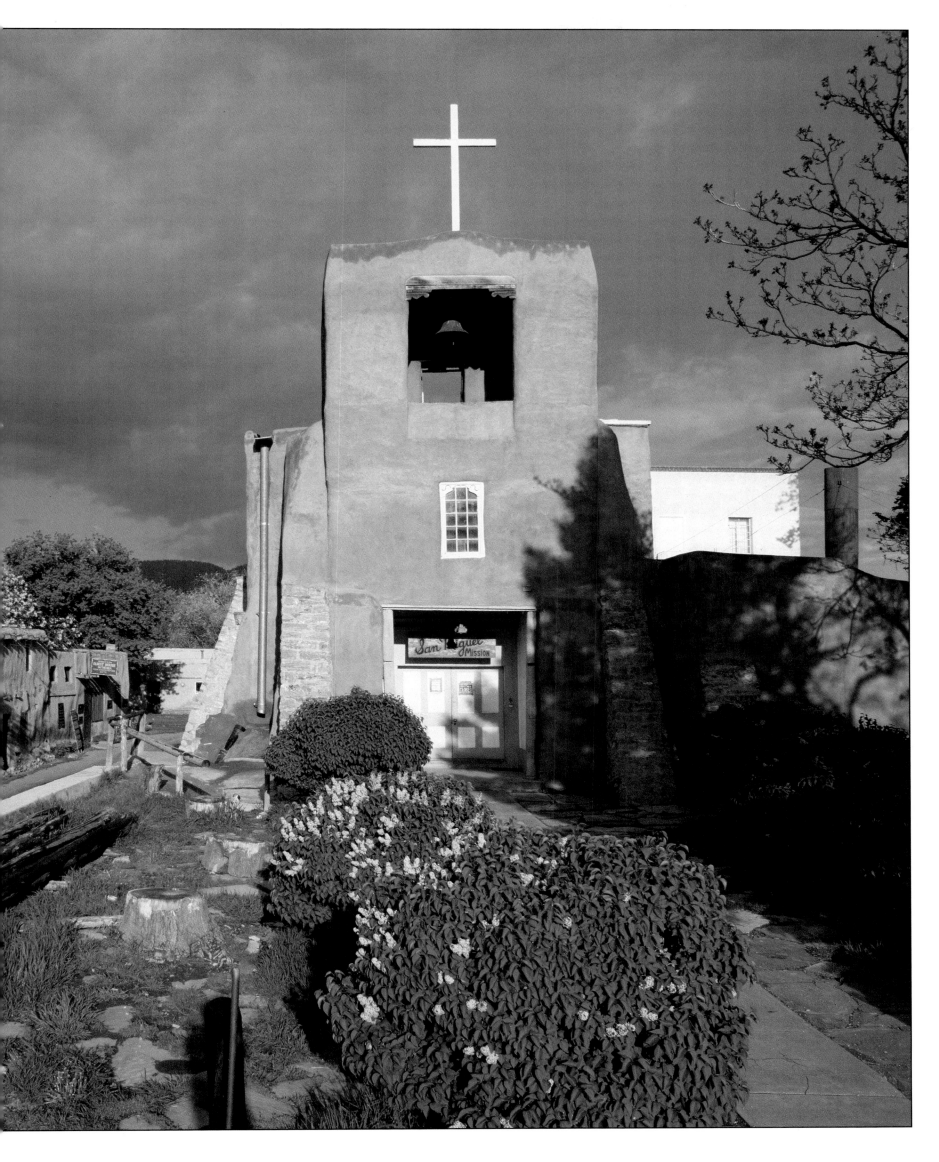

2 cups grated mild cheese
Salt
Flour for dredging
Oil for deep frying
8 eggs, separated
6 tbsps all-purpose flour
Pinch salt
Finely chopped green onions

METHOD

Blanch the whole peppers in boiling water for about 10-15 minutes, or until just tender. Rinse them in cold water and pat them dry. Carefully cut around the stems to make a top, remove and set aside. Scoop out the seeds and cores, leaving the peppers whole. Leave upside down on paper towels to drain. Mix together the chilies, garlic, sage, cheeses and salt to taste. Fill the peppers using a small teaspoon and replace the tops, sticking them into the filling. Dredge the peppers with flour and heat the oil in a deep fat fryer to 375°F. Beat the egg yolks and flour in a mixing bowl until the mixture forms a ribbon trail when the beaters are lifted. Beat the whites with a pinch of salt until stiff but not dry. Fold into the egg yolk mixture. Shape 2 tbsps of batter into an oval and drop into the oil. Immediately slide a metal draining spoon under the batter to hold it in place. Place on a filled pepper. Cover the tops of the peppers with more batter and then spoon over hot oil to seal. Fry until the batter is brown on all sides, turning the peppers over carefully. Drain on paper towels and keep them warm on a rack in a moderate oven while frying the remaining peppers. Sprinkle with onions and serve with Red Sauce.

NEW ORLEANS JAMBALAYA

An easy and extremely satisfying dish of rice and seafood. Sometimes garlic sausage is added for extra spice.

Preparation Time: 40 minutes
Cooking Time: 25-30 minutes
Serves: 4-6

INGREDIENTS

2 tbsps butter or margarine
2 tbsps flour
1 medium onion, finely chopped
1 clove garlic, crushed
1 red pepper, seeded and finely chopped
14oz canned tomatoes
4 cups fish or chicken stock
¼ tsp ground ginger
Pinch allspice
1 tsp chopped fresh thyme or ½ tsp dried thyme
¼ tsp cayenne pepper
Pinch salt
Dash tabasco
4oz uncooked rice
2lbs uncooked shrimp, peeled
2 green onions, chopped to garnish

METHOD

Melt the butter in a heavy-based saucepan and then add the flour. Stir to blend well and cook over low heat until a pale straw color. Add the onion, garlic and pepper and cook until soft. Add the tomatoes and their juice, breaking up the tomatoes with a fork or a potato masher. Add the stock and mix well. Add the ginger, allspice, thyme, cayenne pepper, salt and tabasco. Bring to the boil and allow to boil rapidly, stirring for about 2 minutes. Add the rice, stir well and cover the pan. Cook for about 15-20 minutes, or until the rice is tender and has absorbed most of the liquid. Add the shrimp during the last 10 minutes of cooking time. Cook until the shrimp curl and turn pink. Adjust the seasoning, spoon into a serving dish and sprinkle with the chopped green onion to serve.

FETTUCINE ESCARGOTS WITH LEEKS AND SUN-DRIED TOMATOES

These dried tomatoes keep for a long time and allow you to add a sunny taste to dishes whatever the time of year.

Preparation Time: 15-20 minutes
Serves: 4-6

INGREDIENTS

6 sun-dried tomatoes or 6 fresh Italian plum tomatoes
14oz canned escargots (snails), drained
12oz fresh or dried whole-wheat fettucine (tagliatelle)
3 tbsps olive oil
2 cloves garlic, crushed
1 large or 2 small leeks, trimmed, split, well washed and finely sliced
6 oyster, shittake or other large mushrooms
4 tbsps chicken or vegetable stock
3 tbsps dry white wine

Above: Cheese or Vegetable Enchiladas.

6 tbsps heavy cream
2 tsps chopped fresh basil
2 tsps chopped fresh parsley
Salt and pepper

METHOD

To "sun-dry" tomatoes in the oven, cut the tomatoes in half lengthwise. Use a teaspoon or your finger to scoop out about half the seeds and juice. Press gently with your palm to flatten slightly. Sprinkle both sides with salt and place tomatoes, cut side up, on a rack over a baking pan. Place in the oven on the lowest possible setting, with door ajar, if neccessary, for 24 hours, checking after 12 hours. Allow to dry until no liquid is left and the tomatoes are firm. Chop roughly. Drain the escargots well and dry with paper towels. Place the fettucine in boiling salted water and cook for about 10-12 minutes, or until al dente. Drain, rinse under hot water and leave in a colander to drain dry. Meanwhile, heat the olive oil in a frying pan and add the garlic and leeks. Cook slowly to soften slightly. Add the mushrooms and cook until the leeks are tender crisp. Remove to a plate. Add the drained escargots to the pan and cook over high heat for about 2 minutes, stirring constantly. Pour on the stock and wine and bring to the boil. Boil to reduce by about a quarter and add the cream and tomatoes. Bring to the boil then cook slowly for about 3 minutes. Add the herbs, salt and pepper to taste. Add the leeks, mushrooms and fettucine to the pan and heat through. Serve immediately.

CHEESE OR VEGETABLE ENCHILADAS

Many dishes in Southwestern cooking have Mexican origins, like these tortillas filled with achoice of cheese or spicy vegetable fillings.

Preparation Time: 1 hour
Cooking Time: 23-28 minutes
Serves: 4

INGREDIENTS

8 Tortillas (see recipe)
Full quantity Red Sauce (see Southwestern Stir-fry)

CHEESE FILLING

2 tbsps oil
1 small red pepper, seeded and finely diced
1 clove garlic, crushed
1 tbsp chopped fresh coriander
½ cup heavy cream
½ cup cream cheese
½ cup mild cheese, grated
Whole coriander leaves

VEGETABLE FILLING

2 tbsps oil
1 small onion, finely chopped

1 green pepper, seeded and diced
2 zucchini, diced
½ tsp oregano
½ tsp ground cumin
4oz corn, fresh or frozen
Salt and pepper
1½ cups grated mild cheese
Sour cream
Full quantity green chili salsa (see Gulf Coast Tacos)

METHOD

Prepare the tortillas, red sauce and green chili salsa according to the recipe directions. Heat the oil for the cheese filling and cook the pepper and garlic slowly to soften. Add the coriander and pour in the cream. Bring to the boil and cook rapidly to thicken. Add the cream cheese and stir to melt. Add the grated mild cheese, stir in and keep the filling warm. Re-heat the tortillas wrapped in foil in a moderate oven for about 10 minutes. Place one at a time on serving dishes and spoon in the cheese filling. Fold over both sides to the middle. Re-heat the red sauce, if necessary, and spoon over the center of two enchiladas. Garnish with coriander leaves. For the vegetable filling, heat the oil and cook the onion to soften. Add the remaining vegetables except the corn. Add the oregano and cumin and cook about 3 minutes or until the onions are soft. Add the corn and heat through, adding seasoning to taste. Stir in the grated cheese and fill the tortillas as before, but place in a baking dish. Cook, covered, for about 10-15 minutes at 350°F, or until the cheese has melted and the filling is beginning to bubble. Serve topped with sour cream and green chili salsa.

SALAD HUEVOS RANCHEROS

Chicory is becoming popular all over the United States. This recipe puts it to delicious use with eggs and other Southwestern favorites — peppers, zucchini, jicama and chorizo.

Preparation Time: 45 minutes
Cooking Time: 16 minutes

Serves: 4

INGREDIENTS

4 heads chicory
1 large red pepper, roasted (see Chicken with Red Peppers)
1 large or 2 small zucchini, cut into matchstick pieces
1 small jicama root, cut into matchstick pieces
2-3 green onions, shredded
1 chorizo sausage, blanched and cut into thin strips
4 eggs
4 tbsps pine nuts

DRESSING

1 tsp chopped fresh coriander
6 tbsps oil
2 tbsps lime juice
Dash tabasco
Salt and pinch sugar

METHOD

Prepare the roasted pepper and cut it into thin strips. Blanch the chorizo as for Indian Bread Chorizo and Salsa. Separate the leaves of the chicory and slice or leave whole if small. Bring water to the boil and blanch the zucchini and jicama strips for one minute. Rinse under cold water until completely cool and leave to drain. Combine with the chicory. Add the strips of chorizo and set aside. Toast the pine nuts in a moderate oven until golden brown, about 5 minutes. Bring at least 2 inches of water to the boil in a frying or sauté pan. Turn down the heat to simmering. Break an egg onto a saucer or into a cup. Stir the water to make a whirlpool and then carefully pour the egg into the center, keeping the saucer or cup close to the level of the water. When the water stops swirling and the white begins to set, gently move the egg over to the side and repeat with each remaining egg. Cook the eggs until the whites are completely set, but the yolks are still soft. Remove the eggs from the water with a draining spoon and place them immediately into a bowl of cold water. Mix the dressing ingredients together and pour half over the vegetables and sausage. Toss to coat. Arrange the mixture on individual plates in the shape of nests. Remove the eggs from the cold water with the draining spoon and hold them over a towel for a few minutes to drain completely. Place one egg in the middle of each nest. Spoon the remaining dressing over each egg, sprinkle over the pine nuts and garnish the yolk with a coriander leaf.

BRUNCH SCRAMBLED EGGS

A dash of paprika makes a pretty garnish for these delicious scrambled eggs. They go nicely with Brunch Cheese Grits.

Preparation Time: 10 minutes
Cooking Time: 10 minutes
Serves: 4-6

INGREDIENTS

2 tbsps butter
6 eggs, slightly beaten
¾ cup cottage cheese, drained
2 tbsps milk or cream
1 tbsp chives, chopped
Pinch marjoram leaves
Pinch cayenne pepper
½ tsp salt

Left: Brunch Scrambled Eggs.

METHOD

Gently mix together the eggs, cottage cheese, milk and seasonings. Melt the butter over a low heat in a heavy skillet. Add the egg mixture and cook slowly, turning the mixture with a spatula when it begins to thicken.

DORIS BELCHER, MEMPHIS, TN

SPICY ORIENTAL NOODLES

A most versatile vegetable dish, this goes well with meat or stands alone for a vegetarian main course.

Preparation Time: 25 minutes
Cooking Time: 7-8 minutes
Serves: 4

INGREDIENTS

8oz Chinese noodles (medium thickness)
5 tbsps oil
4 carrots, peeled
8oz broccoli
12 Chinese mushrooms, soaked 30 minutes
1 clove garlic, peeled
4 green onions, diagonally sliced
1-2 tsps chili sauce, mild or hot
4 tbsps soy sauce
4 tbsps rice wine or dry sherry
2 tsps cornstarch

METHOD

Cook noodles in boiling salted water for about 4-5 minutes. Drain well, rinse under hot water to remove starch and drain again. Toss with about 1 tbsp of the oil to prevent sticking. Using a large, sharp knife or Chinese cleaver, slice the carrots thinly on the diagonal. Cut the flowerets off the stems of the broccoli and divide into even-sized but not too small sections. Slice the stalks thinly on the diagonal. If they seem tough, peel them before slicing. Place the vegetables in boiling water for about 2 minutes to blanch. Drain and rinse under cold water to stop the cooking, and leave to drain dry. Remove and discard the mushroom stems and slice the caps thinly. Set aside with the onions. Heat a wok and add the remaining oil with the garlic clove. Leave the garlic in the pan while the oil heats and then remove it. Add the carrots and broccoli and stir-fry about 1 minute. Add mushrooms and onions and continue to stir-fry, tossing the vegetables in the pan continuously. Combine chili sauce, soy sauce, wine and cornstarch, mixing well. Pour over the vegetables and cook until the sauce clears. Toss with the noodles and heat them through and serve immediately.

Below: the bright lights of Las Vegas. Facing page: Spicy Oriental Noodles.

DENVER OMELET

This is a quick and easy meal for busy people or unexpected company. If prepared like scrambled eggs, the mixture can double as a sandwich filling.

Preparation Time: 25 minutes
Cooking Time: 10-15 minutes
Serves: 2

INGREDIENTS

4 strips bacon, diced
Half a small onion, chopped
Half a small green pepper, seeded and chopped
1 tomato, seeded and diced
3 eggs, beaten
Salt and pepper
1 tbsp grated cheese
Dash tabasco (optional)
Chopped parsley to garnish

METHOD

Heat a medium-size frying pan or omelet pan. Add the bacon and sauté slowly until the fat is rendered. Turn up the heat and cook until the bacon begins to brown and crisp. Add the onion and green pepper to soften and finish off the bacon. Mix the tomato with the eggs, salt, pepper, cheese and tabasco, if using. Pour into the pan and stir once or twice with a fork to mix all the ingredients. Cook until lightly browned on the underside. Place under a pre-heated broiler and cook the top quickly until brown and slightly puffy. Sprinkle with parsley, cut into wedges and serve immediately.

Left: the picture postcard surroundings of Dream Lake, Rocky Mountain National Park, Colorado. Above: Denver Omelet.

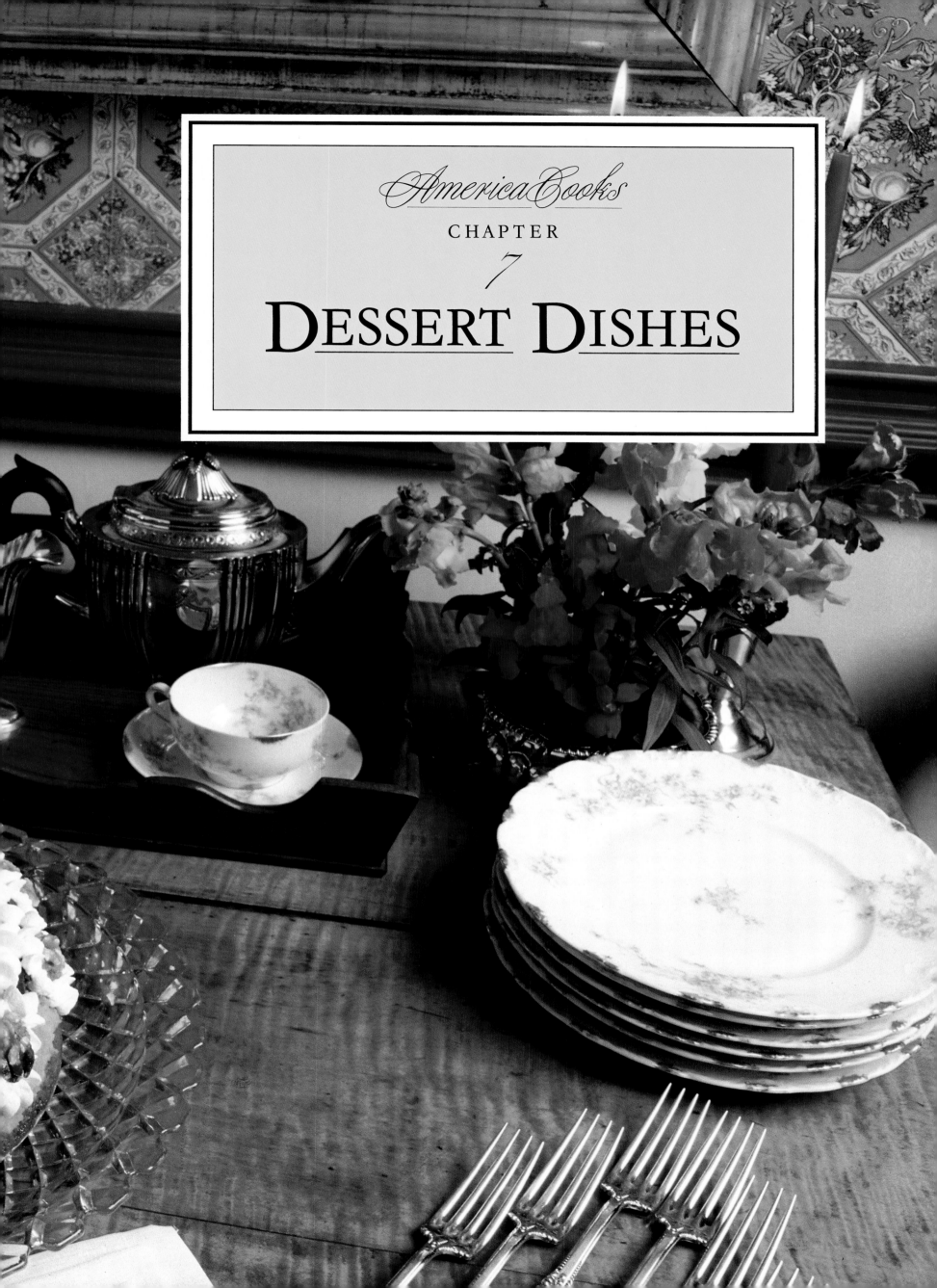

America Cooks

CHAPTER

7

DESSERT DISHES

Previous pages:
Pumpkin Cheesecake.

PUMPKIN CHEESECAKE

An interesting way of using pumpkin is to combine it with cream cheese in a deliciously rich cheesecake. Try it as an alternative to pumpkin pie for Thanksgiving dinner.

Preparation Time: 20 minutes
Cooking Time: 1 hour 50 minutes
Oven Temperature: 325°F
Makes: 1 cake

INGREDIENTS

CHEESECAKE CRUST

1 cup graham cracker crumbs
¼ cup brown sugar
½ cup melted butter or margarine

PUMPKIN FILLING

4 8oz packages cream cheese, softened
1 cup granulated sugar
½ cup brown sugar, packed
5 eggs, beaten
2 cups canned pumpkin
2 tsps pumpkin pie spice
1 tsp vanilla

DECORATION

Whipped cream
Cherries
Walnuts
Fresh mint

METHOD

Combine the ingredients for the cheesecake crust and mix well. Press into a 9 inch spring-form pan and bake for 8-10 minutes at 425°F. Place the cream cheese in a mixing bowl and beat in the sugar until the mixture is light and fluffy. Add the beaten eggs gradually and mix in the remaining ingredients. Pour on top of the crust in the spring-form pan and lower the oven temperature to 325°F. Bake for 1 hour 20 minutes, or until the cake is firm around the edges. Turn off the heat and let the cake remain in the oven an additional 30 minutes. Cool on a rack completely before removing from the tin. Garnish the top with whipped cream, cherries, walnuts and fresh mint leaves.

BERNADETTE CHOUINARD,
DANVILLE, VT

Right: Blueberry Pie.

BLUEBERRY PIE

Americans love pie for dessert. In New England, where blueberries flourish, it's only natural to find them in a pie.

Preparation Time: 30-40 minutes
Cooking Time: 50-55 minutes
Makes: 1 Pie

INGREDIENTS

Double quantity pastry for Pumpkin Pie recipe

FILLING

1lb blueberries
2 tbsps cornstarch
4 tbsps water
2 tbsps lemon juice
1 cup sugar
1 egg beaten with a pinch of salt

Facing page: Persimmon
Pudding.

METHOD

Prepare the pastry in the same way as for the Pumpkin Pie recipe. Divide the pastry in half and roll out one half to form the base. Use a floured rolling pin to lower it into the dish, and press it against the sides. Chill the pastry in the dish and the remaining half of the pastry while preparing the filling. Place the fruit in a bowl and mix the cornstarch with the water and lemon juice. Pour it over the fruit, add the sugar and mix together gently. Spoon the fruit filling into the pastry base. Roll out the remaining pastry on a lightly-floured surface and cut it into strips. Use the strips to make a lattice pattern on top of the filling and press the edges to stick them to the pastry base. Cut off any excess pastry. Using your fingers or a fork, crimp the edges to decorate. Brush the crimped edge of the pastry and the lattice strips lightly with the beaten egg and bake in a pre-heated 425°F oven for about 10 minutes. Reduce the heat to 350°F and bake for a further 40-45 minutes. Serve warm or cold.

PERSIMMON PUDDING

A rich and satisfying pudding for autumn made with this plump, bright orange fruit. Spice it up with preserved or fresh ginger.

Preparation Time: 25 minutes
Cooking Time: 45 minutes
Serves: 6

INGREDIENTS

2-4 ripe persimmons or Sharon fruit (depending on size)
4 tbsps honey
Juice and rind of 1 small orange
1 egg
½ cup light cream
¾ cup all-purpose flour
½ tsp baking powder
½ tsp baking soda

Pinch cinnamon and nutmeg
2 tbsps melted butter
1 small piece preserved ginger, finely chopped, or small
piece freshly grated ginger
4 tbsps chopped walnuts or pecans
Whipped cream, orange segments and walnut or pecan
halves to garnish

ORANGE SAUCE

1 cup orange juice
Sugar to taste
1 tbsp cornstarch
2 tbsps brandy or orange liqueur

METHOD

Peel the persimmons or Sharon fruit by dropping them into boiling water for about 5 seconds. Remove to a bowl of cold water and leave to stand briefly. This treatment makes the peels easier to remove. Scoop out any seeds and purée the fruit until smooth. Add the honey, orange juice and rind, egg and cream, and process once or twice. Pour the mixture into a bowl. Sift the flour, baking powder, baking soda and spices over the persimmon purée and gradually fold together. Stir in the melted butter, ginger and nuts and spoon into well buttered custard cups. Place in a bain marie and bake until risen and set, about 45 minutes, in a pre-heated 350°F oven. Test by inserting a skewer into the middle. If the skewer comes out clean the puddings are set. Allow to cool slightly. Combine the sauce ingredients and cook slowly, stirring continuously, until thickened and cleared. Stir in the brandy or orange liqueur. When the puddings have cooled slightly, loosen them from the edge of the dish and turn out onto a plate. Spoon some of the sauce over each and garnish with whipped cream, orange segments and nuts.

CHARLOTTE

This elegant and delicious dessert will grace any dinner party table.

Preparation Time: 30 minutes
Cooking Time: approximately 10 minutes
Serves: 8-10

INGREDIENTS

2 tbsps unflavored gelatin
¼ cup cold water
2 cups milk
4 eggs, separated
½ cup sugar
⅛ tsp salt
2 tbsps whiskey
1 pint whipping cream
1 dozen lady fingers

METHOD

In a mixing bowl, sprinkle the gelatin over the cold water and leave to soak until all of the gelatin is moist. Heat the milk to just below boiling and set aside to cool slightly. Meanwhile, separate the eggs and beat the yolks slightly. Add the sugar and salt, followed by a small amount of the hot milk. Stir well. Add this mixture to the remaining hot milk and cook over a low heat, stirring constantly, until the mixture coats the back of the spoon. Pour this mixture over the gelatin in the mixing bowl and stir until the gelatin is dissolved. Cool, then add the whiskey. When the mixture begins to gel, beat the egg whites until stiff, but still moist. Fold the egg whites into the custard by cutting a spoon through the egg whites and custard

Left: Charlotte.

and turning the custard over the egg whites. Blend in this manner until no lumps of egg white are visible. Beat the cream until stiff and fold into the mixture in the same way as the egg whites. Line a mold with lady fingers and spoon the custard mixture on top. Cover and chill thoroughly.

To serve, unmold and top with additional whipped cream.

STURDIVANT MUSEUM ASSOCIATION,
SELMA, AL

FRUIT TART

This dessert is really a combination of pie and fruit crisp. The base is a variation of French pie pastry and the topping bakes crisp and sweet. It is delicious with any seasonal fruit.

Preparation Time: 25-30 minutes
Cooking Time: 30 minutes
Oven Temperature: 350°F
Makes: 1 pie

INGREDIENTS

CRUST
1 cup flour
3 tbsps sugar
¼ tsp baking powder
4 tbsps cold butter
1 egg
6 drops almond extract

FILLING
3 cups fruit such as peaches, blueberries, strawberries
or apples
Lemon juice

TOPPING
2 tbsps flour
2 tbsps sugar
3 tbsps butter
Pinch cinnamon

METHOD

Combine the flour, sugar and baking powder in a food processor and process once or twice to sift. Add the butter and cut in until the mixture resembles fine bread crumbs. Add the egg and the almond extract and mix to bring the pastry together. Press into a pie plate evenly over the bottom and sides. Prepare the fruit and sprinkle lemon juice over. Pile the fruit into the pastry and set it aside. Melt the butter for the topping and stir in the remaining ingredients. Sprinkle over the fruit and bake for 30 minutes in a moderate oven, or until the crust is brown and the fruit is tender and bubbling.

DANIEL ROUTHIER,
DEAN'S MILL FARM,
STONINGTON, CT

BLACK BOTTOM ICE CREAM PIE

Unbelievably simple, yet incredibly delicious and impressive, this pie is a perfect ending to a summer meal or a spicy one anytime.

Preparation Time: 25 minutes
Makes: 1 pie

Facing page: Fruit Tart, photographed at the home of Arnold Copper, Stonington.

Left: Black Bottom Ice Cream Pie.

INGREDIENTS

8-10 Graham crackers, crushed
½ cup butter or margarine, melted
3 cups coffee ice cream
2oz semi-sweet chocolate, melted
4oz shredded coconut
Dark rum

METHOD

Crush crackers with a rolling pin or in a food processor. Mix with melted butter or margarine. Press into an 8 ½ inch false-bottomed flan dish. Chill thoroughly in the refrigerator. Meanwhile, combine 4 tbsps coconut with the melted chocolate. When cooled but not solidified, add about a quarter of the coffee ice cream, mixing well. Spread the mixture on the base of a crust and freeze until firm. Soften the remaining ice cream with an electric mixer or food processor and spread over the chocolate-coconut layer. Re-freeze until firm. Toast the remaining coconut in a moderate oven, stirring frequently until pale golden brown. Allow to cool completely. Remove the pie from the freezer and leave in the refrigerator 30 minutes before serving. Push up the base of the dish and place the pie on a serving plate. Sprinkle the top with toasted coconut. Cut into wedges and drizzle with rum before serving.

FRUIT MERINGUE CHANTILLY

During the 19th century in the United States, individual meringues were very popular and much enjoyed at teatime. Meringues are not difficult to make; just be sure that the whites are beaten to stiff peaks before any sugar is added.

Preparation Time: 30 minutes
Cooking Time: 1 hour
Oven Temperature: 275°F
Serves: 8-10

INGREDIENTS

1½ cups egg whites
¾ tsp cream of tartar
Pinch salt
2 ¼ cups granulated sugar
1 kiwi fruit, peeled
1 fresh pineapple, peeled and cored
¾ cup green seedless grapes
½ cup seeded purple grapes
3 navel oranges, peeled and segmented
1 banana, sliced and dipped in lemon or orange juice
3 cups heavy cream, whipped with ¾ cup
powdered sugar
2 tsps vanilla extract
2 squares German sweet chocolate

METHOD

Let the egg whites warm to room temperature (1 hour). Beat the egg whites with the cream of tartar and a pinch of salt at a high speed. Once stiff peaks form, gradually beat in the granulated sugar, making sure the meringue mixture is stiff between each addition of sugar. Lightly grease and flour two baking sheets and drop the meringues with a spoon about 1¼ inches apart. Bake in a preheated oven for approximately 1 hour or until crisp. The meringues should stay pale in color. Remove to a wire rack to cool while preparing the fruit.

   Cut the fruit into small pieces, leaving ⅓ in larger pieces for garnish. Fold the cut fruit into the whipped cream. Build

Right: Flourless
Chocolate Cake.

the meringues in a tree formation using the fruit and cream mixture to hold the meringues together. Garnish with the remaining fruit and sprinkle with grated chocolate.

PATRICIA McLAUGHLIN,
THE LOBSTER POUND RESTAURANT,
LINCOLNVILLE BEACH, ME

FLOURLESS CHOCOLATE CAKE

This is part mousse, part soufflé, part cake and completely heavenly! It's light but rich, and adored by chocolate lovers everywhere.

Serves: 6

INGREDIENTS

1lb semi-sweet chocolate
2 tbsps strong coffee
2 tbsps brandy
6 eggs
6 tbsps sugar
1 cup whipping cream
Powdered sugar
Fresh whole strawberries

METHOD

Melt the chocolate in the top of a double boiler. Stir in the coffee and brandy and leave to cool slightly. Break up the eggs and then, using an electric mixer, gradually beat in the sugar until the mixture is thick and mousse-like. When the beaters are lifted the mixture should mound slightly. Whip the cream until soft peaks form. Beat the chocolate until smooth and shiny, and gradually add the egg mixture to it. Fold in the cream and pour the cake mixture into a well greased 9″ deep cake pan with a disk of wax paper in the bottom. Bake in a pre-heated 350°F oven in a bain marie. To make a bain marie, use a roasting pan and fill with warm water to come halfway up the side of the cake pan. Bake about 1 hour and then turn off the oven, leaving the cake inside to stand for 15 minutes. Loosen the sides of the cake carefully from the pan and allow the cake to cool completely before turning it out. Invert the cake onto a serving plate and carefully peel off the paper. Place strips of wax paper on top of the cake, leaving even spaces in betweeen the strips. Sprinkle the top with powdered sugar and carefully lift off the paper strips to form a striped or chequerboard decoration. Decorate with whole strawberries.

FOUR-LAYERED CHEESECAKE

The chopped almonds and shredded coconut that form the base of this cheesecake make a delightful change from the graham cracker crust found on most cheesecakes. Also, this crust couldn't be simpler. Various flavors in the layers combine beautifully to make a cheesecake that tastes as good as it looks.

Preparation Time: 30 minutes
Cooking Time: 1 hour 55 minutes
Oven Temperature: 425°F reduced to 225°F
Makes: 1 10-inch cake

INGREDIENTS

½ cup butter, softened
¾ cup each of chopped almonds and shredded coconut

FILLING

3lbs cream cheese
4 eggs
½ cup flour
1 cup confectioners' sugar
½ cup dark bittersweet chocolate, melted
½ cup cognac
½ cup almond paste
½ cup Amaretto

Below: Four-Layered Cheesecake.

½ cup praline paste
½ cup Frangelico
½ cup white chocolate, melted
2 tbsps vanilla
½ cup rum

METHOD

Grease the inside of a 10″ springform pan generously with the softened butter. Dust the pan with a mixture of almonds and coconut. Press the mixture against the butter to help it stick. Combine the cream cheese, eggs, flour and confectioners' sugar and beat until well mixed. Divide the mixture into quarters and add to one quarter the melted dark chocolate and the cognac. Pour this mixture into the pan on top of the crust. To the second quarter, add the almond paste and amaretto and mix well. Carefully spread across the first layer. To the third quarter, add the praline paste and Frangelico. Blend again and lightly spread on top of the last layer. To the final quarter, add the melted white chocolate, vanilla and rum. Pour this over the top and carefully spread out. Place in the oven at 425°F for 15 minutes; reduce to 225°F and bake for another hour and 45 minutes. Remove and allow to cool completely before refrigerating. Chill for 24 hours before serving. Decorate the top with chocolate leaves.

JAMES HALLER'S KITCHEN,
PORTSMOUTH, NH

FRESH FRUIT COBBLER

Serve this tempting dessert warm with cream or whipped cream. You can vary the fruit to suit the season.

Preparation Time: 30 minutes

Cooking Time: 30 minutes
Serves: 6-8

INGREDIENTS

¾-1 cup sugar
1 tbsp cornstarch
1 cup water
3½ cups sliced fresh fruit (for example apples, peaches or berries, plus juice)
½ tbsp butter
Pinch cinnamon

PASTRY

1 cup all-purpose flour
⅓ tsp salt
⅓ cup plus 1 tbsp shortening
2-3 tbsps cold water
½ tbsp butter, melted
Pinch cinnamon

METHOD

Combine the sugar, cornstarch and water and bring to a boil. Boil for 1 minute, then add the fruit and juice and cook for a further minute. Pour into a well buttered 1½-quart baking dish. Sprinkle lightly with the cinnamon and dot with the butter. Prepare the pastry by combining the flour and salt. Cut in the shortening until the mixture resembles coarse crumbs. Sprinkle in the water and mix gently until the dough can be formed into a soft ball. Roll out on a floured surface to a ⅛-inch thickness. Cut the dough into ½-inch-wide strips and arrange in a lattice pattern over the fruit. Brush the pastry with melted butter, sprinkle with cinnamon and bake at 400°F for 30 minutes, or until the cobbler is golden brown and bubbly.

DORIS BELCHER, MEMPHIS, TN

Facing page: the boiling waters of the Beaver River, Minnesota.

Left: Fresh Fruit Cobbler.

PUMPKIN PIE

American Indians taught the settlers about the pumpkin and it was one of the crops that helped to save their lives.

Preparation Time: 30 minutes
Cooking Time: 50-60 minutes
Makes: 1 Pie

INGREDIENTS

PASTRY

1 cup all-purpose flour
Pinch salt
¼ cup butter, margarine or lard
Cold milk

PUMPKIN FILLING

1lb cooked and mashed pumpkin
2 eggs
1 cup evaporated milk
½ cup brown sugar
1 tsp ground cinnamon
¼ tsp ground allspice
Pinch nutmeg
Pecan halves for decoration

METHOD

To prepare the pastry, sift the flour and a pinch of salt into a mixing bowl. Rub in the fat until the mixture resembles fine breadcrumbs. Stir in enough cold milk to bring the mixture together into a firm ball. Cover and chill for about 30 minutes before use. Roll out the pastry on a lightly-floured surface to a circle about 11 inches in diameter. Wrap the pastry around a lightly-floured rolling pin and lower it into a 10 inch round pie dish. Press the pastry into the dish and flute the edge or crimp with a fork. Prick the base lightly with the tines of a fork. Combine all the filling ingredients in a mixing bowl and beat with an electric mixer until smooth. Alternatively, use a food processor. Pour into the pie crust and bake in a pre-heated 425°F oven. Bake for 10 minutes at this temperature and then lower the temperature to 350°F and bake for a further 40-50 minutes, or until the filling is set. Decorate with a circle of pecan halves.

PEARS IN ZINFANDEL

Zinfandel has a spicy taste that complements pears beautifully.

Preparation Time: 25 minutes
Cooking Time: 50 minutes
Serves: 6

INGREDIENTS

3 cups Zinfandel or other dry red wine
1 cup sugar
1 cinnamon stick
1 strip lemon peel
6 Bosc pears, even sized
4 tbsps sliced almonds
1 tbsp cornstarch mixed with 3 tbsps water
Mint leaves to garnish

METHOD

Pour the wine into a deep saucepan that will hold 6 pears standing upright. Add the sugar, cinnamon and lemon peel, and bring to the boil slowly to dissolve the sugar. Stir occasionally. Peel pears, remove 'eye' on the bottom, but leave

Left: the *Memphis Queen III* on the Mississippi near Memphis.

Above: Pears in Zinfandel.

Facing page: Cranberry Pudding.

INGREDIENTS

Favorite recipe for a 10-inch 1-crust pastry shell

FILLING
2 cups puréed butternut squash
2 whole eggs, beaten
1 cup sugar
¾ cup milk
½ cup heavy cream
¼ tsp salt
½ tsp each ginger, nutmeg, cinnamon and allspice
1 tsp grated lemon rind
1 tsp lemon juice
4oz butter, melted and cooled

WALNUT TOPPING
3 tbsps brown sugar
2 tbsps butter
1 tbsp milk
½ cup chopped walnuts

METHOD

Mix all the filling ingredients together well and pour into the unbaked prepared pie shell. Bake until a skewer inserted into the center of the filling comes out clean, about 1 hour 45 minutes. Before the pie cools, combine the topping ingredients and melt over gentle heat. Spoon over the pie and allow to cool completely before cutting to serve.

CRANBERRY PUDDING

This is a steamed pudding in the English tradition, made American by the use of cranberries and brought up-to-date by the addition of wheatgerm and honey.

Preparation Time: 25 minutes
Cooking Time: 1½ hours
Serves: 8

INGREDIENTS

1½ cups sliced cranberries
3 tbsps sugar
1½ cups whole-wheat flour
2 tsps baking powder
½ tsp salt
1 tbsp milk powder
¼ cup wheatgerm
2 eggs, well beaten
½ cup honey
⅓ cup milk

LEMON SAUCE
½ cup sugar
3 tsps cornstarch
1 cup boiling water
Juice and rind of 1 lemon
1 tbsp butter

METHOD

Place the cranberries and sugar in a bowl and leave to stand. Place all the dry ingredients in a large bowl and mix the liquid ingredients separately. Gradually add the liquid ingredients to the dry ingredients, stirring well. Fold in the cranberries and spoon into a well greased 2 pint pudding bowl or pudding basin. Cover with a sheet of wax paper and then seal the bowl or basin well with foil or a lid. Place on a rack in a pan of simmering water. Cover the pan and steam for 1½ hours. Check the level of the water occasionally and add more water if necessary.

on the stems. Stand the pears close together in the wine, so that they remain standing. Cover the pan and poach gently over low heat for about 25-35 minutes, or until tender. If the wine does not cover the pears completely, baste the tops frequently as they cook. Meanwhile, toast almonds on a baking sheet in a moderate oven for about 8-10 minutes, stirring them occasionally for even browning. Remove and allow to cool. When pears are cooked, remove from the liquid to a serving dish. Boil the liquid to reduce it by about half. If it is still too thin to coat the pears, thicken it with 1 tbsp cornstarch dissolved in 3 tbsps water. Pour syrup over the pears and sprinkle with almonds. Serve warm or refrigerate until lightly chilled. Garnish pears with mint leaves at the stems just before serving.

SQUASH PIE WITH WALNUT TOPPING

This is delicious change from the traditional pumpkin pie.

Preparation Time: 25 minutes
Cooking Time: 1 hour 45 minutes
Oven Temperature: 350°F
Makes: 1 10-inch pie

Meanwhile, prepare the lemon sauce. Mix the sugar and cornstarch together in a saucepan and stir in the boiling water gradually. Add the rind and juice of the lemon and bring to the boil. Stir constantly until thickened and cleared. Beat in the butter and serve warm with the pudding. If preparing the sauce in advance, place a sheet of wax paper or plastic film directly over the sauce to prevent a skin forming on the surface.

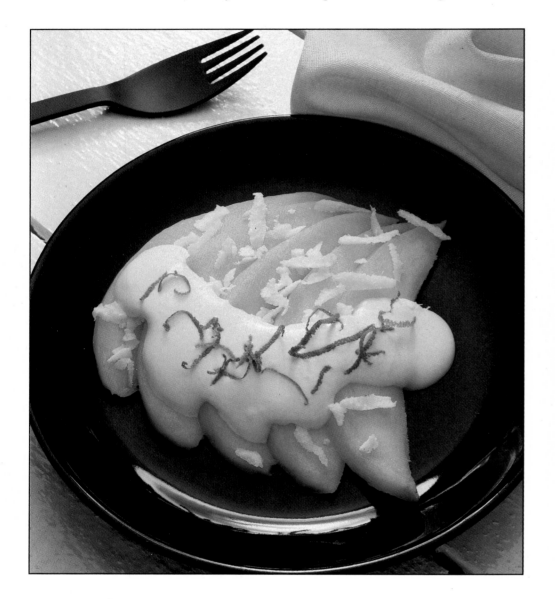

Right: Ala Moana Park, Oahu, Hawaii. Above: Mango and Coconut with Lime Sabayon – a delicious blend of exotic fruit.

MANGO AND COCONUT WITH LIME SABAYON

The taste of mango with lime is sensational, especially when served with the deliciously creamy sauce in this stylish dessert.

Preparation Time: 40 minutes
Cooking Time: 8 minutes
Serves: 4

INGREDIENTS

2 large, ripe mangoes, peeled and sliced
1 fresh coconut
2 egg yolks
4 tbsps sugar
Juice and grated rind of 2 limes
½ cup heavy cream, whipped

METHOD

Arrange thin slices of mango on plates. Break coconut in half and then into smaller sections. Grate the white pulp, taking care to avoid grating the brown skin. Use the coarse side of

Facing page: Fresh
Raspberries with Cream.

the grater to make shreds and scatter them over the mango slices. Place egg yolks and sugar in the top of a double boiler or a large bowl. Whisk until very thick and lemon colored. Stir in the lime juice and place mixture over simmering water. Whisk constantly while the mixture gently cooks and becomes thick and creamy. Remove from the heat and place in another bowl of iced water to cool quickly. Whisk the mixture while it cools. Fold in the whipped cream and spoon onto the fruit. Garnish with the grated lime rind.

GUAVA MINT SORBET

When a light dessert is called for, a sorbet can't be surpassed. The exotic taste of guava works well with mint.

Preparation Time: 2-3 hours including freezing
Makes: 3 cups

INGREDIENTS

4 ripe guavas
⅔ cup granulated sugar
1 cup water
2 tbsps chopped fresh mint
1 lime
1 egg white
Fresh mint leaves for garnish

METHOD

Combine the sugar and water in a heavy-based saucepan and bring slowly to the boil to dissolve the sugar. When the mixture is a clear syrup, boil rapidly for 30 seconds. Allow to cool to room temperature and then chill in the refrigerator. Cut the guavas in half and scoop out the pulp. Discard the peels and seeds and purée the fruit until smooth in a food processor. Add the mint and combine with cold syrup. Add lime juice until the right balance of sweetness is reached. Pour the mixture into a shallow container and freeze until slushy. Process again to break up ice crystals and then freeze until firm. Whip the egg white until stiff but not dry. Process the sorbet again and when smooth, add the egg white. Mix once or twice and then freeze again until firm. Remove from the freezer 15 minutes before serving and keep in the refrigerator. Scoop out and garnish each serving with mint leaves.

FRESH RASPBERRIES WITH CREAM

This is a simply prepared dessert with eye-appeal and lots of flavor. Any fresh berry or combination of berries lends itself easily to this recipe.

Preparation Time: 15 minutes

Right: Guava Mint
Sorbet.

Right: Wizard Island in Crater Lake, Crater Lake National Park, Oregon.

Serves: 6

INGREDIENTS

3 cups fresh raspberries or a combination
of different berries
1½ pints fresh heavy cream

METHOD

Select the raspberries or other berries as fresh as possible. Pick over and discard bruised or damaged berries. Rinse only if absolutely necessary. Arrange the berries carefully in stemmed glass dessert dishes. Drizzle each serving with 2fl oz of heavy cream and serve.

CHEF STEPHEN MONGEON,
THE RED LION INN,
STOCKBRIDGE, MA

APPLE PANCAKE

These apple pancakes are similar to ones prepared in Germany and also have something in common with the French fruit and batter pudding called clafoutis.

Preparation Time: 30 minutes
Cooking Time: 25-28 minutes
Oven Temperature: 375°F reduced to 350°F
Serves: 6

INGREDIENTS

2½ cups all-purpose flour
2oz shortening
8 eggs
1 pint buttermilk
1¾ tsps salt
1¾ tsps sugar
1¾ tsps baking soda
1½ tbsps baking powder
1 tbsp vanilla extract
1 tsp ground cinnamon
⅛ tsp ground nutmeg
2 tbsps melted butter
2 large MacIntosh apples, peeled, cored and diced
1 large MacIntosh apple, peeled, cored and sliced

GLAZE

6oz pure maple syrup
4 tbsps apple cider
2 tbsps melted butter
½ cup dark brown sugar

METHOD

Combine all the dry ingredients and add the shortening, eggs, buttermilk, vanilla, cinnamon, nutmeg and melted butter. With a wooden spoon, mix all the ingredients together. Do not over-mix; the mixture should look lumpy. Add the 2 diced apples and fold into the mixture. Allow to stand for 15 minutes before cooking.

Meanwhile, make the glaze. Combine the butter and cider over a low heat and add the sugar, maple syrup and mix well. Lightly brush 6½" French crêpe pans with softened butter. Heat in the oven for 3 minutes. Remove the pans from the oven and ladle in about 6 fl oz of the batter, bringing it to within a ¼ inch of the top of the pan. Decorate each pancake with 4 of the reserved apple slices. Return to the oven for a further 10 minutes. Reduce the heat to 350°F and bake for 15-18 minutes, or until a skewer comes out clean from the center when tested. Remove from the oven and allow to stand for

5 minutes. Loosen the pancake from the edges and slide out onto a warm plate. Lightly brush with glaze and serve the remaining glaze separately. Serve with fruit such as a strawberry fan or an orange twist, if desired. The pancake can also be prepared in one large skillet and sliced into wedges to serve.

CHEF STEPHEN MONGEON,
THE RED LION INN,
STOCKBRIDGE, MA

FROZEN LIME AND BLUEBERRY CREAM

Preparation Time: 40 minutes plus freezing overnight
Serves: 6

INGREDIENTS

Juice and rind of 4 limes
Water
1 cup sugar
4oz blueberries
3 egg whites
1 cup heavy cream, whipped

METHOD

Measure the lime juice and make up to 6 tbsps with water if necessary. Combine with the sugar in a heavy-based pan and bring to the boil slowly to dissolve the sugar. When the mixture forms a clear syrup, boil rapidly to 250°F on a sugar thermometer. Meanwhile, combine the blueberries with about 4 tbsps water in a small saucepan. Bring to the boil and then simmer, covered, until very soft. Purée, sieve to remove the seeds and skin, and set aside to cool. Whisk the egg whites until stiff but not dry and then pour on the hot sugar syrup in a steady stream, whisking constantly. Add the lime rind and allow the meringue to cool. When cold, fold in the whipped cream. Pour in the purée and marble through the mixture with a rubber spatula. Do not over-fold. Pour the mixture into a lightly-oiled mold or bowl and freeze until firm. Leave 30 minutes in the refrigerator before serving or dip the mold for about 10 seconds in hot water. Place a plate over the bottom of the mold, invert and shake to turn out. Garnish with extra whipped cream, blueberries or lime slices.

ORANGE BREAD PUDDING

Bread puddings came to America from England and they remain as popular as ever in both countries.

Facing page: Frozen Lime and Blueberry Cream.

Below: Orange Bread Pudding.

Preparation Time: 30 minutes
Cooking Time: 1½ hours

INGREDIENTS

4 cups milk
8 slices white bread, crusts removed
4 tbsps butter or margarine
6 egg yolks
3 egg whites
1 tbsp orange flower water
¾ cup sugar
½ tsp freshly ground nutmeg
Pinch salt
½ cup orange marmalade

METHOD

Heat the milk until just scalded. In a large bowl, break the bread into cubes and add the butter. Stir in the hot milk until the butter is melted and the bread has broken up. Allow the mixture to cool to luke-warm. Lightly grease a large soufflé dish or pudding basin. Combine the egg yolks and whites with the orange flower water in a bowl, and beat until frothy. Stir in the sugar, nutmeg and salt. Stir the egg mixture into the bread and milk mixture until just combined, and pour into the prepared mold. Cover the mold with lightly greased foil and tie tightly. Place the dish on a rack in a large saucepan and fill with boiling water to within 1 inch of the top of the bowl. Bring the water to boiling and then allow to simmer, covered, for 1½ hours, or until the pudding is firm in the center. Allow to cool for about 30 minutes and then loosen the edge with a knife. Invert onto a serving plate to unmold. Spread the top with orange marmalade and serve warm or cold.

STAINED GLASS DESSERT

Named for the effect of the cubes of colorful gelatine in the filling, this pretty and light pudding can be made well in advance of serving.

Preparation Time: 35-40 minutes plus setting time
Serves: 6-8

INGREDIENTS

3oz each of three fruit-flavored gelatine (assorted)
2 cups Graham crackers, crushed
6 tbsps sugar
½ cup butter or margarine
3 tbsps unflavored gelatine
4 tbsps cold water
3 eggs, separated
6 tbsps sugar
4oz cream cheese
Juice and rind of 1 large lemon
½ cup whipping cream

METHOD

Prepare the flavored gelatines according to package directions. Pour into 3 shallow pans and refrigerate until firm. Mix the crushed Graham cracker with the sugar in a food processor and pour melted butter through the funnel with the machine running to blend thoroughly. Press half the mixture into an 8 inch springform pan lined with wax paper. Refrigerate until firm. Reserve half the mixture for topping. Sprinkle the gelatine onto the water in a small saucepan and allow to stand until spongy. Heat gently until the gelatine dissolves and the

liquid is clear. Combine the egg yolks, lemon juice and sugar and beat until slightly thickened. Beat in the cream cheese a bit at a time. Pour in the gelatine in a thin, steady stream, beating constantly. Allow to stand, stirring occasionally until beginning to thicken. Place in a bowl of ice water to speed up the setting process. Whip the cream until soft. Whip the egg whites until stiff peaks form and fold both the cream and the egg whites into the lemon-cream cheese mixture when the gelatine has begun to thicken. Cut the flavored gelatines into cubes and fold carefully into the cream cheese mixture. Pour onto the prepared crust. Sprinkle the remaining crust mixture on top, pressing down very carefully. Chill overnight in the refrigerator. Loosen the mixture carefully from the sides of the pan, open the pan and unmold. Slice or spoon out to serve.

APPLE TORTE

Serve this delicious dessert warm or cold with vanilla ice cream.

Preparation Time: 20 minutes
Cooking Time: 45 minutes

Serves: 6-8

INGREDIENTS

⅔ cup flour, sifted
3 tsps baking powder
½ tsp salt
2 eggs, beaten
1½ cups sugar
3 tsps vanilla
2 cups apples, peeled, cored and diced
1 cup pecans or walnuts, chopped

METHOD

Preheat the oven to 350°F. Sift together the flour, baking powder and salt. Set aside. In a separate bowl, combine the sugar, vanilla and beaten eggs. Stir in the dry ingredients, apples and nuts. Pour the batter into a buttered 8x12x4-inch baking dish. Bake for 45 minutes or until a knife inserted in the center comes out clean.

RIDGEWELL CATERER, INC.
WOODLAWN PLANTATION COOK BOOK,
JOAN SMITH, EDITOR,
MOUNT VERNON, VA

Above: Stained Glass Dessert.

Facing page: Apple Torte.

STRAWBERRY CHEESECAKE

A cheesecake is a dessert that never fails to please. This recipe serves a large gathering, but can easily be cut in half. Strawberries are a favorite choice for topping and they complement the velvety texture so well. For shine, melt a little seedless raspberry jam and brush over the berries, if desired.

Preparation Time: 30 minutes
Cooking Time: 40 minutes
Oven Temperature: 375°F
Makes: 2-10 inch cakes

INGREDIENTS

3lbs cream cheese or curd cheese
15 eggs
½ cup sour cream
1 tbsp vanilla extract

GRAHAM CRACKER CRUST

4 cups graham cracker crumbs
1⅓ cups sugar
½lb butter, melted

TOPPING

1lb even-sized strawberries, hulled

METHOD

Soften the cream cheese and gradually beat in the eggs. Stir in the sour cream and vanilla extract. Combine the crust ingredients in a food processor or bowl and mix thoroughly. Press into spring-form pans and pour in the filling. Cook in a moderate oven for 40 minutes. Allow to cool completely before removing from the pans. Decorate the top of each cake with strawberries and brush over jam, if desired.

PETER T. CROWLEY,
LA FORGE CASINO RESTAURANT,
NEWPORT, RI

CUSTARD VANILLA ICE CREAM

Preparation Time: 20 minutes
Cooking Time: 10 minutes
Chilling time: at least 3 hours
Yield: 1 gallon

INGREDIENTS

1 cup sugar
1½ tbsps flour
½ gallon milk, scalded
½ pint whipping cream
6 eggs, beaten
14oz can sweetened condensed milk
1 tbsp vanilla
6 Goo Goo Clusters, crumbled
or chocolate peanut candies

METHOD

Combine the flour and sugar in a heavy saucepan. Gradually stir in the scalded milk and the whipping cream. Cook over a medium heat, stirring constantly until thickened, then continue to cook for a further 2 minutes. Remove from the heat and add the condensed milk and vanilla. Chill for at least two

Left: Strawberry Cheesecake.

Above: Bread Pudding with Whiskey Sauce, a dessert with the unmistakable taste of fine Kentucky bourbon.

Facing page: St. Joseph's Cathedral, Bardstown, Kentucky.

hours, then fold in the crumbled Goo Goo Clusters. Freeze the mixture in a 1-gallon ice cream freezer according to the manufacturer's instructions.

If you can bear to wait, this ice cream has the best flavor if allowed to "ripen" or stand for 2 hours before serving. To do this, pack the ice cream freezer with additional ice and salt, then insulate with covers of newspaper or old quilts.

ANN COX, MURFREESBORO, TN

BREAD PUDDING WITH WHISKEY SAUCE

A childhood pudding made sophisticated by the addition of a bourbon-laced sauce, and a stylish presentation.

Preparation Time: 40 minutes
Cooking Time: 35-40 minutes
Serves: 8

INGREDIENTS

½ loaf day-old French bread
2 cups milk
3 eggs
¾ cup raisins
1 tsp vanilla extract
Pinch ground ginger
Butter or margarine
½ cup butter
1 cup sugar
1 egg
4 tbsps bourbon
Nutmeg

METHOD

Cut bread into small pieces and soak in the milk. When the bread has softened, add the eggs, raisins, vanilla and ginger. Grease 8 custard cups with butter or margarine and fill each with an equal amount of pudding mixture to within ½ inch of the top. Place the dishes in a roasting pan and pour in enough hot water to come halfway up the sides of the dishes. Bake in a preheated 350°F oven until risen and set – about 35-40 minutes. When the puddings have cooked, combine the ½ cup butter and the sugar in the top of a double boiler and heat to dissolve the sugar. Beat the egg and stir in a spoonful of the hot butter mixture. Add the egg to the double boiler and whisk over heat until thick. Allow to cool and add bourbon. To serve, turn out puddings onto plates and surround with sauce. Sprinkle the tops with nutmeg.

Right: Nelly Custis'
Maids of Honor.

NELLY CUSTIS' MAIDS OF HONOR

These popular treats originally came from England, but were very popular in early America.

Preparation Time: 20 minutes
Cooking Time: 45 minutes
Yield: 8-10 tarts

INGREDIENTS

Pastry to line 8-10 3½-inch tart pans
2 eggs
½ cup sugar
½ cup almond paste
1-2 tbsps sherry
2 tbsps melted butter
1 tbsp lemon juice
2 tbsps flour
8-10 tsps strawberry or raspberry jam

METHOD

Preheat the oven to 350°F. Use the pastry to line the tart pans and arrange them on a baking sheet. Beat the eggs until very light and fluffy. Gradually beat in the sugar. Soften the almond paste with the sherry, butter and lemon juice. Add this mixture to the beaten eggs. Drop 1 teaspoon of jam into each tart shell and fill with the batter. Bake for about 45 minutes, or until puffed, golden and firm.

RIDGEWELL CATERER, INC.
WOODLAWN PLANTATION COOK BOOK,
JOAN SMITH, EDITOR,
MOUNT VERNON, VA

CHOCOLATE CREAM PIE

Don't expect any leftovers when you serve this irresistible creation!

Preparation Time: 45 minutes
Cooking Time: 25 minutes
Serves: 1 9-inch pie

INGREDIENTS

1 pre-baked 9-inch pie shell
1 cup sugar
¼ cup cocoa
¼ cup cornstarch
¼ tsp salt
3 cups milk
3 egg yolks
1 tsp vanilla extract

MERINGUE TOPPING

3 egg whites
½ tsp vanilla
¼ tsp cream of tartar
6 tbsps sugar

METHOD

To prepare the filling, combine the sugar, cocoa, cornstarch and salt in a heavy saucepan. Mix together the milk and egg yolks and gradually stir into the sugar mixture. Cook over a medium heat, stirring constantly, until the mixture thickens and boils. Continue to cook and stir for 1 minute, then remove from the heat and add the vanilla. Pour the hot filling into

Preparation Time: 20 minutes
Cooking Time: 8-10 minutes
Serves: 6-8

INGREDIENTS

10oz raw lamb, ground
1 onion, minced
1 clove garlic, finely chopped
¼ tsp chopped fresh ginger
½ tsp garam masala
1 tsp lemon juice
1 tbsp chickpea or cornflour
¼-½ pint plain yogurt

METHOD

Make sure the lamb is finely ground. Add the onion and all the remaining ingredients except the yogurt. Knead on a pastry board like bread dough. Shape onto skewers in sausage shapes. Baste with the plain yogurt and place under a broiler or over hot coals. Baste and turn as they cook. When well done, they will come off the skewers easily. Serve with the remaining yogurt, if desired.

ROBERT T. ALLAN,
ASSISTANT EXECUTIVE CHEF,
SHERATON PLYMOUTH INN, MA

LEG OF LAMB ROASTED IN A REFLECTOR OVEN

Lamb is an ideal meat to cook by this method because its natural fat keeps the meat moist. The meat is at its best when it is slightly pink in the center. Rosemary complements the flavor of lamb well, but try thyme or mint for a taste variation.

Preparation Time: 15 minutes
Cooking Time: 1-1½ hours
Serves: 6-8

INGREDIENTS

5-6lb leg of lamb
4 cloves garlic, halved or quartered depending upon size
Fresh or dried rosemary, crushed

METHOD

Push a sharp knife into the meat at 5 inch intervals and insert slivers of garlic into the cuts. Rub with rosemary. Pierce the leg with a skewer and place it in the oven. Cook in front of a slow fire at a distance of approximately 18 inches. Turn every 15 minutes while basting in its own juices. When the meat looks done, cut a small, deep slice to check the color.

STEVEN P. MACK, CHASE HILL FARM,
ASHAWAY, RI

PLANTATION RIB-EYE ROAST WITH MUSHROOM GRAVY

Preparation Time: 15 minutes

Left: Leg of Lamb Roasted in a Reflector Oven, photagraphed at Stephen Mack's Chase Hill Farm, coastal Rhode Island.

Bottom right: a Southwestern stew with a difference, Chili Verde combines the cool smoothness of avocados with the fire of chilis. Facing page: tomatoes, peppers and baby corn provide color as well as taste in Southwestern Stir-Fry.

Cooking Time: 2 hours
Serves: 10-12

INGREDIENTS

8-9lb rib-eye roast
Cracked peppercorns
Garlic salt
Rosemary

MUSHROOM GRAVY

2 tbsps pan drippings from the roast
2 tbsps flour
1 tbsp butter
1 cup fresh mushrooms, sliced
1 cup dry red wine
1 cup beef broth

METHOD

Preheat the oven to 500°F. To cook the roast, rub the meat all over with the peppercorns, garlic salt and rosemary. Arrange the roast in a shallow pan and place in the oven. Cook the roast for 5-6 minutes per pound, then turn off the oven, but do not open the door. Leave the roast in the closed oven for a total of two hours. When you open the oven, the roast will be fully cooked and ready to serve.

To prepare the mushroom gravy, make a roux by blending the drippings, butter and flour in a skillet over a moderate heat. Stir in the mushrooms, then gradually add the broth and red wine. Simmer to allow the gravy to thicken and develop more flavor before serving.

ANN HALL, GREY OAKS,
VICKSBURG, MS

SOUTHWESTERN STIR-FRY

East meets West in a dish that is lightning-fast to cook. Baby corn, traditionally Oriental, echoes the Southwestern love of corn.

Preparation Time: 25 minutes plus 4 hours marinating the meat
Cooking Time: 21-22 minutes
Serves: 4

INGREDIENTS

1lb sirloin or rump steak
2 cloves garlic, crushed
6 tbsps wine vinegar
6 tbsps oil
Pinch sugar, salt and pepper
1 bay leaf
1 tbsp ground cumin
1 small red pepper, seeded and sliced
1 small green pepper, seeded and sliced
2oz baby corn
4 green onions, shredded
Oil for frying

RED SAUCE

8 fresh ripe tomatoes, peeled, seeded and chopped
4 tbsps oil
1 medium onion, finely chopped
1-2 green chilies, finely chopped
1-2 cloves garlic, crushed
6 sprigs fresh coriander
3 tbsps tomato paste

METHOD

Slice the meat thinly across the grain. Combine in a plastic bag with the next 6 ingredients. Tie the bag and toss the ingredients inside to coat. Place in a bowl and leave about 4 hours. Heat the oil for the sauce and cook the onion, chilies and garlic to soften but not brown. Add remaining sauce ingredients and cook about 15 minutes over gentle heat. Purée in a food processor until smooth. Heat a frying pan and add the meat in three batches, discarding the marinade. Cook to brown and set aside. Add about 2 tbsps of oil and cook the peppers about 2 minutes. Add the corn and onions and return the meat to the pan. Cook a further 1 minute and add the sauce. Cook to heat through and serve immediately.

CHILI VERDE

A chili, really a spicy meat stew, is as traditional in the Southwest as it is in Mexico.

Preparation Time: 30-40 minutes
Cooking Time: 1-1½ hours
Serves: 4

INGREDIENTS

2lbs lean pork, cut into 1 inch pieces
Oil
3 green peppers, seeded and cut into 1 inch pieces
1-2 green chili peppers, seeded and finely chopped
1 small bunch green onions, chopped
2 cloves garlic, crushed
2 tsps ground cumin
2 tsps chopped fresh oregano
3 tbsps chopped fresh coriander
1 bay leaf
3 cups beer, water or chicken stock
8oz canned chickpeas, drained

1½ tbsps cornstarch mixed with
3 tbsps cold water (optional)
Salt
1 large ripe avocado, peeled and diced
1 tbsp lime juice

METHOD

Heat 4 tbsps of oil and lightly brown the pork cubes over high heat. Use a large flameproof casserole and brown the pork in 2 or 3 batches. Lower the heat and cook the peppers to soften slightly. Add the chilies, onions, garlic and cumin and cook for 2 minutes. Add the herbs and liquid and reduce the heat. Simmer, covered, 1-1½ hours or until the meat is tender. Add the chickpeas during the last 45 minutes. If necessary, thicken with the cornstarch, stirring constantly after adding until the liquid thickens and clears. Add salt to taste and remove the bay leaf. Toss the avocado in lime juice and sprinkle over the top of the chili to serve.

COUNTRY HAM WITH BOURBON RAISIN SAUCE

The tart and sweet flavor of this sauce, with its added 'kick' of bourbon, has long been the choice to complement savory country ham.

Preparation Time: 20 minutes
Cooking Time: 2 minutes per side of ham
Serves: 4 or 8

INGREDIENTS

8 slices country or Smithfield ham, cut about ¼ inch thick
Milk
Oil or margarine for frying

SAUCE

1½ tbsps cornstarch
1 cup apple cider
½ tsp ginger or allspice
2 tsps lemon juice
2 tbsps bourbon
2oz raisins
Pinch salt

METHOD

Soak the ham slices in enough milk to barely cover for at least 30 minutes. Rinse and pat dry. Trim off the rind and discard it. Heat a small amount of oil or margarine in a large frying pan and brown the ham slices about 2 minutes per side over medium-high heat. Mix the cornstarch with about 6 tbsps of the apple cider and deglaze the frying pan with the remaining cider. Stir in the ginger or allspice and the lemon juice. Stirring constantly, pour in the cornstarch mixture and bring the liquid to the boil. Cook and stir constantly until thickened. Add the bourbon and raisins and cook a further 5 minutes. Add salt to taste. Reheat the ham quickly, if necessary, and pour over the sauce to serve.

CHILI ROJA

Red meat, red onions, red peppers, paprika, tomatoes and red beans all give clues to the name of this zesty stew.

Preparation Time: 25 minutes

Right: the Grand Canyon and Colorado River seen from Lipan Point, Arizona.

Facing page: Alabama
Cola Glazed Ham.

Cooking Time: 1½-2 hours
Serves: 6-8

INGREDIENTS

2lbs beef chuck, cut into 1 inch pieces
Oil
1 large red onion, coarsely chopped
2 cloves garlic, crushed
2 red peppers, seeded and cut into 1 inch pieces
1-2 red chilies, seeded and finely chopped
3 tbsps mild chili powder
1 tbsp cumin
1 tbsp paprika
3 cups beer, water or stock
8oz canned tomatoes, puréed
2 tbsps tomato paste
8oz canned red kidney beans, drained
Pinch salt
6 ripe tomatoes, peeled, seeded and diced

METHOD

Pour about 4 tbsps oil into a large saucepan or flameproof casserole. When hot, brown the meat in small batches over moderately high heat for about 5 minutes per batch. Set aside the meat on a plate or in the lid of the casserole. Lower the heat and cook the onion, garlic, red peppers and chilies for about 5 minutes. Add the chili powder, cumin and paprika and cook for 1 minute further. Pour on the liquid and add the canned tomatoes, tomato paste and the meat. Cook slowly for about 1½-2 hours. Add the beans about 45 minutes before the end of cooking time. When the meat is completely tender, add salt to taste and serve garnished with the diced tomatoes.

ALABAMA COLA GLAZED HAM

Don't be afraid to try this somewhat unusual approach to roast ham. Cola gives it a marvelous taste and color.

Preparation Time: 30 minutes plus overnight soaking
Cooking Time: 2 hours 15 minutes
Serves: 8-10

INGREDIENTS

10lb joint country or Smithfield ham
4 cups cola soft drink
Whole cloves
1 cup packed dark brown sugar

METHOD

Soak the ham overnight. Preheat oven to 350°F. Place the ham rind side down in a roasting pan. Pour over all but 6 tbsps of the cola and bake, uncovered, 1½ hours or until the internal temperature registers 140°F. Baste the ham every 20 minutes with pan juices using a large spoon or a bulb baster. Remove the ham from the oven and allow it to cool for 10-15 minutes. Remove the rind from the ham with a small, sharp knife and score the fat to a depth of ¼ inch. Stick 1 clove in the center of every other diamond. Mix sugar and the remaining cola together and pour or spread over the ham. Raise the oven temperature to 375°F. Return the ham to the oven and bake for 45 minutes, basting every 15 minutes. Cover loosely with foil if the ham begins to brown too much. Allow to stand 15 minutes before slicing.

Right: Chili Roja.

the pre-baked pie shell. To make the topping, beat the egg whites and the cream of tartar at room temperature using an electric mixer at high speed. Add the sugar, a tablespoon at a time, and continue to beat until stiff peaks form and the sugar is dissolved. Spread the meringue over the hot filling right to the edge of the pastry to form a seal. Bake at 350°F for 12-15 minutes, or until the meringue is golden brown. Cool before serving.

ELSIE WALKER, SPRINGFIELD, TN

AVONDALE SWANS

Use a simple-to-make pastry to make a delightfully imaginative dessert. Fruit purées, chocolate or fudge sauces go well with these ice cream-filled swans. In the Olympia Tea Room, the swans are served swimming in a pool of espresso-flavored chocolate sauce.

Preparation Time: 30 minutes
Cooking Time: 20-30 minutes
Oven Temperature: 400°F
Makes: 3-4 swans

INGREDIENTS

PÂTE A CHOUX
½ cup boiling water
¼ cup butter, cut in small pieces
½ cup all-purpose flour, sifted
2 eggs (at room temperature

FILLING
Ice cream
Whipped cream

METHOD

To prepare the pastry, add the butter to boiling water and stir to melt completely. Blend in the flour and stir to make a stiff dough. Allow to cool slightly and beat in 1 egg at a time until thoroughly blended. Beat until the mixture is smooth and satiny and of thick dropping consistency. It may not be necessary to use all the egg.

To shape the swans, use a small ice cream scoop or spoon to place rounded mounds of the mixture on a baking sheet. Use ¾ of the mixture to shape the bodies of the swans. The swans will take 20-30 minutes to bake, depending on size. Shape the necks and heads by placing the remaining pastry in a pastry bag with a straight, narrow tip. Squeeze out the pastry making a backwards S with a rounded beginning. Bake these separately as they will take less time than the bodies.

To assemble the swans, allow the pastry to cool and cut off the top ⅓ of each body. Split this piece in half; these halves become the wings. Scoop out any soft pastry from the inside of the shells and fill with ice cream. Cover the ice cream with whipped cream, insert the wings and neck into the ice cream and serve the swans swimming in a pool of your favorite sauce.

THE OLYMPIA TEA ROOM,
BAY STREET, WATCH HILL, RI

MAPLE SYRUP MOUSSE

Pure maple syrup is a true delicacy. It isn't cheap, but the flavor it gives special recipes like this mousse makes it worth its price.

Preparation Time: 30 minutes

Cooking Time: 10 minutes
Serves: 4-6

INGREDIENTS

4 eggs, separated
2 extra egg whites
¾ cup maple syrup
1 cup heavy cream
Chopped pecans or walnuts to decorate

METHOD

Place the syrup in a saucepan and bring to the boil. Continue boiling to reduce the syrup by one quarter. Beat the egg yolks until thick and lemon colored. Pour the maple syrup onto the egg yolks in a thin, steady stream, beating with an electric mixer. Continue beating until the mixture has cooled. Beat the egg whites until stiff but not dry and whip the cream until soft peaks form. Fold the cream and egg whites into the maple mixture and spoon into a serving bowl or individual glasses. Refrigerate until slightly set and top with chopped walnuts or pecans to serve.

LEMON CHESS PIE

No one is really sure how this zesty lemon and cornmeal pie came to be so named, but it's delicious nonetheless.

Preparation Time: 30 minutes
Cooking Time: 45 minutes

Above: Maple Syrup Mousse, a delicious way of enjoying Vermont's famous maple syrup.

Facing page: Avondale Swans, photographed at Stephen Mack's Chase Hill Farm, coastal Rhode Island.

Serves: 6

INGREDIENTS

1½ cups all-purpose flour
Pinch salt and sugar
6 tbsps butter or margarine
2 tbsps plus 1 tsp vegetable shortening
4-5 tbsps cold water

FILLING

4 tbsps softened butter
1 cup sugar
3-4 eggs, depending on size
1 tbsp yellow cornmeal
Rind and juice of 1 lemon

METHOD

Sift the flour, salt and sugar into a bowl or process once or twice in a food processor. Add the butter or margarine and shortening and rub into the flour until the mixture resembles fine breadcrumbs, or use the food processor. Add enough water to bring the mixture together in a firm dough. Knead lightly to eliminate cracks, wrap and chill for 30 minutes while preparing the filling. Cream the butter with the sugar until the sugar dissolves. Add the eggs, one at a time, beating well in between each addition. Stir in the cornmeal, rind and juice of the lemon. Roll out the pastry in a circle on a well-floured surface. Roll the pastry carefully onto the rolling pin and transfer to a 9 inch pie or flan dish. Lower the pastry carefully into the dish and press against the sides and base. Trim the edges with a sharp knife if using a pie dish, or roll over the rim of the flan dish with the rolling pin to cut off the excess. Pour in the filling and bake at 350°F for about 45 minutes. Lower the temperature to 325°F if the pie begins to brown too quickly. Cook until the filling sets. Allow to cool completely before serving. Sprinkle lightly with powdered sugar before cutting, if desired.

JEFFERSON DAVIS PIE

Named in honor of one of the heroes of the Confederacy, this pie is sure to please.

Preparation Time: 20 minutes
Cooking Time: 50-60 minutes
Serves: 8

INGREDIENTS

1 tbsp flour
1 tbsp cornmeal
2 cups sugar
4 eggs
¼ cup butter, melted
¼ cup lemon juice
1 tbsp grated lemon rind
¼ cup milk
1 9-inch unbaked pie shell

METHOD

Sift the flour and cornmeal into the sugar. Beat the eggs slightly and add to the sugar mixture, blending well. Add the butter, lemon juice, lemon rind and milk. Pour this filling into the unbaked pie shell. Bake at 350°F for 50-60 minutes or until the filling is set and the center is firm.

MARTIN LAFFEY,
DELTA POINT RIVER RESTAURANT,
VICKSBURG, MS

Left: Jefferson Davis Pie.

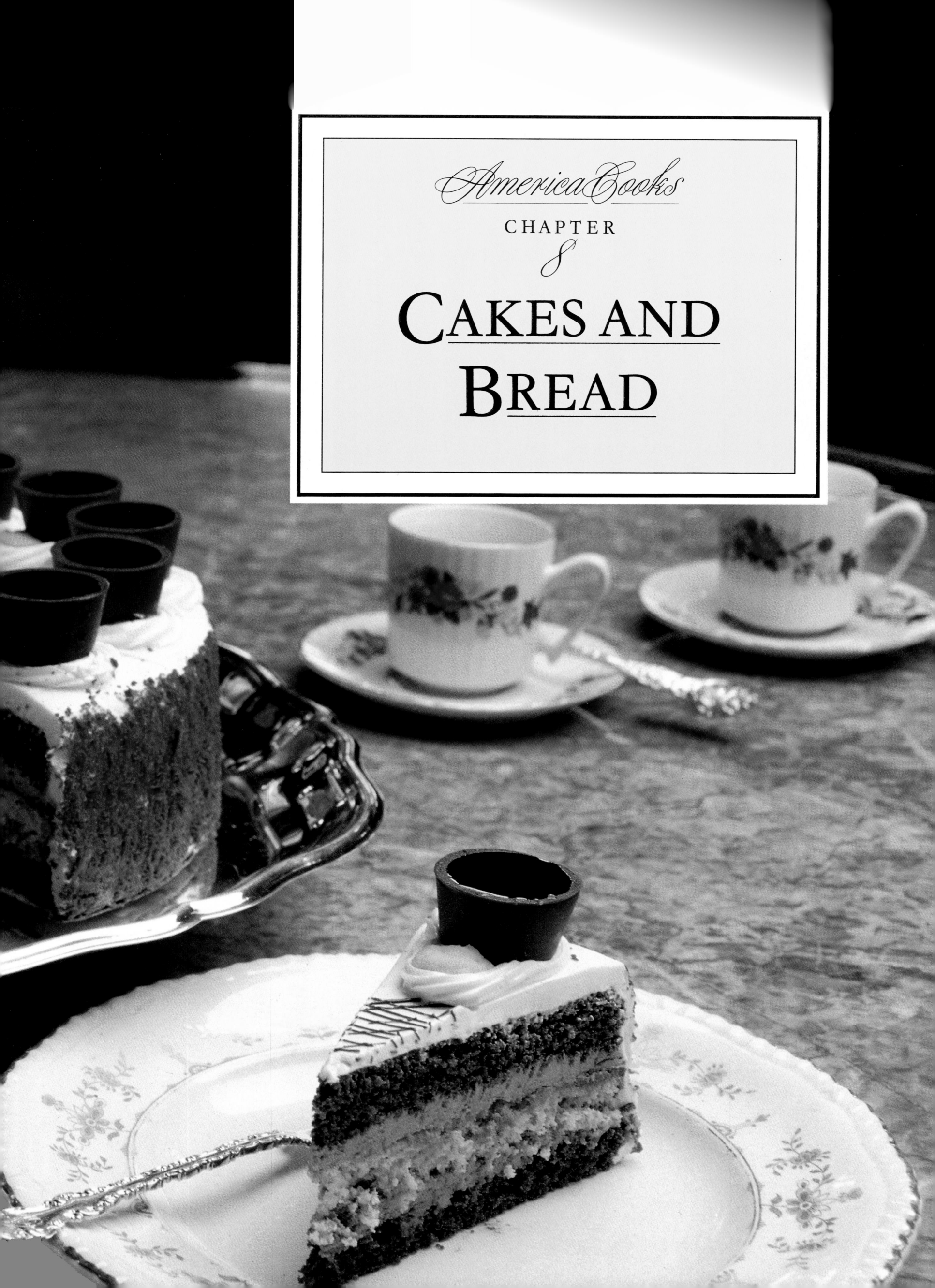

America Cooks

CHAPTER
8

CAKES AND
BREAD

Previous pages: Grand
Marnier Cake.

GRAND MARNIER CAKE

Preparation Time: 1 hour
Cooking Time: 20-30 minutes
Oven Temperature: 375°F
Serves: 8

INGREDIENTS

CAKE

2¼ cups sugar
12 eggs, separated
2¼ cups unsalted butter, melted
¾ cup all-purpose flour sifted with a pinch of salt
Pinch cream of tartar
6oz German sweet chocolate

CHOCOLATE CUPS

2oz semi-sweet baking chocolate
1 tsp shortening
Grand Marnier

ICING

2lbs unsalted butter
1 cup shortening
1 cup milk
2 cups powdered sugar, sifted
1 tsp vanilla
2oz dark chocolate, melted

METHOD

First grease and flour 3 8-inch round cake pans. Beat the sugar and egg yolks together until thick and lemon colored. Fold in the melted butter and sift in the flour, salt and cream of tartar. Fold together to mix thoroughly. Beat the egg whites until stiff but not dry. Fold into the cake mixture carefully. Do not over fold. Divide the mixture in thirds and fill 2 of the prepared cake pans with ⅔ of the mixture. Fold the melted chocolate into the remaining third and spoon into the remaining pan. Bake in a moderate oven until the mixture shrinks slightly from the sides of the pans and the tops spring back when touched lightly.

Meanwhile, prepare the chocolate cups. Chop the chocolate into small pieces and combine with the shortening in the top of a double boiler. Melt over gently simmering water, stirring occasionally. When the chocolate is melted, use a pastry brush to paint an even layer of chocolate in each of 8 paper candy cups. Allow to harden, chilling in the refrigerator if necessary.

While the cakes are cooling, prepare the icing. Beat the butter and shortening until light and fluffy. Sift in the powdered sugar and beat until creamy, adding the milk gradually. It may not be necessary to add all the milk. Melt the chocolate and allow it to cool slightly before adding it to ⅓ of the icing. Add vanilla to the remaining ⅔ of the icing.

To assemble the cake, cut the 3 layers in half, horizontally. Sandwich the layers together, alternating the chocolate and vanilla icings, saving enough vanilla icing for the top and sides of the cake. Peel the paper cups carefully away from the chocolate and fill each chocolate cup with Grand Marnier.

PETER T. CROWLEY,
LA FORGE CASINO RESTAURANT,
NEWPORT, RI

Right: Hazelnut
Florentines.

HAZELNUT FLORENTINES

Preparation Time: 45-50 minutes

Cooking Time: 10 minutes
Makes: 24-30

INGREDIENTS

1lb shelled and peeled hazelnuts
1 cup sugar
6 tbsps honey
6 tbsps heavy cream
1 cup butter
6oz white chocolate, melted
6oz semi-sweet chocolate, melted

METHOD

Place hazelnuts in a plastic bag and tie securely. Tap nuts or roll them with a rolling pin to crush roughly. Place sugar, honey, cream and butter in a heavy-based saucepan and heat gently to dissolve sugar. Bring to the boil and cook rapidly for about 1½ minutes. Remove from heat and stir in the nuts. Brush baking sheets well with oil and spoon or pour out mixture in even amounts. Make only about six Florentines at a time. Bake about 10 minutes in a pre-heated 375°F oven. Allow to cool on the baking sheets and, when nearly set, loosen with a spatula and transfer to a flat surface to cool completely. When all Florentines have been baked and cooled, melt both chocolates separately. Spread white chocolate on half of the Florentines and semi-sweet chocolate on the other half, or marble the two if desired. Place chocolate side uppermost to cool slightly and then make a wavy pattern with the tines of a fork, or swirl chocolate with a knife until it sets in the desired pattern.

CHURROS

These fritters can be either sweet or savory. Either way, they're a treat with a Mexican influence.

Preparation Time: 25-30 minutes
Cooking Time: 6 minutes per piece
Makes: 12-14

INGREDIENTS

BASIC DOUGH

Scant 1 cup plus 2 tbsps water
3 tbsps butter or margarine
Pinch salt
1 cup all-purpose flour
6 tbsps cornmeal
2 eggs
Oil for deep frying

SAVORY INGREDIENTS

2 tbsps finely grated cheese
2 chili peppers, seeded and finely chopped
Parmesan cheese (optional)

SWEET INGREDIENTS

4 tbsps sugar
1 tbsp unsweetened cocoa powder
1 tsp ground cinnamon
Powdered sugar (optional)

METHOD

Combine the water, butter or margarine and salt in a heavy-based saucepan. If making sweet churros, add sugar as well. Cook over medium heat until the butter or margarine melts. Immediately stir in the flour and cornmeal. Keeping the pan over medium heat, stir until the mixture pulls away from the sides of the pan and forms a ball. Take off the heat and cool slightly. Add the eggs one at a time, beating vigorously in between each addition. It may not be necessary to add all the egg. Beat until the mixture is smooth and shiny and thick enough to pipe. Add the cheese and chilies *or* the cocoa and cinnamon with the eggs. Spoon the mixture into a pastry bag fitted with a star tip. Heat the oil in a deep fat fryer, deep saucepan or deep sauté pan to a depth of at least 4 inches.

Pipe the dough into the oil in 10 inch strips and fry until golden brown, about 3 minutes per side. Drain on paper towels and sprinkle the savory churros with Parmesan cheese and the sweet with powdered sugar, if desired. Serve warm.

SPICED CRANBERRY NUT BREAD

Sassamanesh was the colorful Indian name for this equally colorful berry. Here, it brightens up a quickly prepared bread.

Preparation Time: 25 minutes
Cooking Time: 1 hour
Makes: 1 loaf

INGREDIENTS

2 cups all-purpose flour
1 tsp baking powder
1 cup sugar
1 tsp baking soda
Pinch salt
¼ tsp ground nutmeg
¼ tsp ground ginger
½ cup orange juice
2 tbsps butter or margarine, melted
4 tbsps water
1 egg
1 cup fresh cranberries, roughly chopped
1 cup hazelnuts, roughly chopped

METHOD

Sift the dry ingredients and spices into a large mixing bowl. Make a well in the center of the dry ingredients and pour in

the orange juice, melted butter or margarine, water and egg. Using a wooden spoon, beat the liquid mixture, gradually drawing in the flour from the outside edge. Add the cranberries and nuts and stir to mix completely. Lightly grease a loaf pan about 9 x 5″. Press a strip of wax paper on the base and up the sides. Lightly grease the paper and flour the whole inside of the pan. Spoon or pour in the bread mixture and bake in a pre-heated 325°F oven for about 1 hour, or until a skewer inserted into the center of the loaf comes out clean. Remove from the pan, carefully peel off the paper and cool on a wire rack. Lightly dust with confectioner's sugar, if desired, and cut into slices to serve.

Right: Georgia Pecan Cake, a rich but absolutely irresistible centerpiece to any dessert selection.

GEORGIA PECAN CAKE

This makes a delicious and spectacular dessert centerpiece.

Preparation Time: 45 minutes
Cooking Time: 35 minutes
Yield: 1 3-layer 9-inch cake

INGREDIENTS

½ cup margarine
½ cup shortening
2¼ cups sugar
5 eggs, separated
2½ cups plain flour
1 tsp soda
1 cup buttermilk
2 tbsps vanilla
½ cup grated coconut
2 cups pecans, chopped

ICING

½ cup margarine
16oz cream cheese
2lbs confectioners' sugar
3 tbsps vanilla
¾ cup pecans, chopped

METHOD

Using an electric mixer, cream together the margarine, shortening and sugar for 15 minutes on medium speed. Add the egg yolks and continue to mix on low for 5 minutes. Sift the flour and soda together 3 times and add to the mixing bowl alternately with the buttermilk, beginning and ending with the flour. Turn off the mixer and fold in the vanilla, coconut and pecans. Beat the egg whites until stiff, and gently fold in the cake batter. Divide the mixture into 3 greased and floured 9-inch cake pans. Bake at 350°F for 30-35 minutes, or until the cake springs back when touched lightly in the center. Cool for 15 minutes on a rack before turning the layers out of the pans and leaving to cool completely. While the cakes are cooling, prepare the icing. Cream together all of the icing ingredients, except for the pecans. When the cakes are completely cool, spread the icing thickly on top of each cake and sprinkle ¼ cup of the chopped pecans on top. Place the cakes on top of each other to make a three layered cake.

SARALYN LATHAM, THE WILLIS HOUSE, MILLEDGEVILLE, GA

SYRUP CAKE

Rather like gingerbread, but with a spicy taste of cinnamon, nutmeg and cloves instead, this cake can be served cool with coffee or tea or warm with cream.

Preparation Time: 20 minutes
Cooking Time: 45 minutes
Makes: 1 cake

INGREDIENTS

1 cup vegetable shortening
1 cup molasses
3 eggs, beaten
3 cups all-purpose flour
1 tbsp baking powder
Pinch salt
1 tsp cinnamon
¼ tsp ground nutmeg
Pinch ground cloves
4 tbsps chopped pecans
4 tbsps raisins

METHOD

Cream the shortening until light and fluffy. Add the molasses and beat with an electric mixer. Add the eggs one at a time, beating well in between each addition. Sift the flour together with a pinch of salt and baking powder. Combine with the molasses mixture and add the spices. Stir in the nuts and raisins and pour the mixture into a lightly greased 9 x 13″ baking pan. Bake for about 45 minutes in a pre-heated 375°F oven. To test for doneness, insert a skewer into the center of the cake. If it comes out clean, the cake is done. Allow to cool and cut into squares to serve.

BEIGNETS

A night on the town in New Orleans is not complete without stopping for chicory coffee and fresh hot beignets.

Preparation Time: 1 hour
Cooking Time: 15 minutes
Yield: 20 beignets

INGREDIENTS

½ cup milk, warmed to blood temperature
2 tsps dried yeast or ⅓oz fresh yeast
1 egg, beaten
⅛ cup sugar
½ tsp salt
1¾ cups bread flour
⅛ cup butter, softened
Oil for deep fat frying
Confectioners' sugar

METHOD

Dissolve the yeast in the warm milk, then add the sugar, salt and beaten egg. Gradually add half of the flour, stirring until well blended, then mix in the softened butter. Gradually add the rest of the flour until the dough is very stiff and can only be mixed with your hands.

Place the dough in a warm bowl and cover with a towel. Leave it to rise in a warm place for approximately 1 hour, or until it has doubled in bulk. Knead gently on a floured surface, then roll out to a ¼-inch thickness. Cut the dough into rectangles approximately 2½ x 3½ inches and place on a lightly floured pan. Cover with a towel and leave to rise for approximately 35 minutes. Deep fry in oil which has been heated to 360°F, turning once when the bottom side has browned. Drain on paper towels, then dust generously with confectioners' sugar.

JOHN D. FOLSE, LAFITTE'S LANDING,
P.O. BOX 1128, DONALDSONVILLE, LA

Right: ornate ironwork on New Orleans' Vieux Carré.
Facing page: Beignets.

America Cooks
INDEX

⅛ *tsp Tabasco sauce*
1lb potatoes, peeled and diced (optional)
Salt and freshly ground black pepper to taste

METHOD

Wash the peas and pick over. Soak in 2½ quarts warm water for 6-8 hours or overnight. Melt the renderings until hot in a large soup pot. Add the onion, carrots, celery, thyme, garlic powder, Worcestershire sauce and Tabasco. Sauté 3-5 minutes or until the vegetables are cooked yet still firm. Place the bay leaves, cloves and peppercorns in a square of cheesecloth and tie to make a small bag. Add the peas and soaking liquid, ham hocks or bone and the cheesecloth bag to the pan and bring the mixture to the boil. Skim off the foam when the mixture comes to the boil. Reduce the heat and simmer gently for 1½ hours. Add the diced potato at this time, if desired, and simmer an additional 30 minutes. Remove the ham hocks or bone and set aside to cool. Remove the meat and discard any fat, sinew and gristle. Dice the lean meat into small cubes. Check the consistency of the soup and, if desired, add more water. If the soup is not thick enough, extend the cooking time. Add the diced ham, adjust the seasonings and serve with the desired garnishes or accompaniments.

CHEF STEPHEN MONGEON,
THE RED LION INN,
STOCKBRIDGE, MA

STUFFED EGGPLANT WITH SHRIMP

Preparation Time: 45 minutes
Cooking Time: 1 hour
Serves: 8

INGREDIENTS

4 medium eggplants
2 tbsps shortening
1 cup chopped onions
1 cup chopped bell pepper
½ cup chopped celery
2 cloves garlic, chopped
½ cup chopped scallions
1lb ground beef
1lb fresh shrimp, chopped
3½ cups seasoned Italian bread crumbs
2 eggs, beaten
Salt and pepper to taste

METHOD

Slice the eggplants lengthwise and place in a pot of lightly salted water. Bring to a rolling boil and cook until tender. Drain, cool and scoop out the flesh, being careful not to tear the shell. Drain the excess water from the flesh and chop finely.

Melt the shortening in a sauté pan over a medium high heat. Sauté the onions, scallions, bell pepper, garlic and celery for approximately five minutes, stirring occasionally. Add the ground beef and blend well into the vegetable mixture. Continue cooking for approximately 20 minutes or until brown. Finally, add the shrimp and chopped eggplant flesh. Cook for about 30 minutes, stirring occasionally to keep from sticking. Add 2½ cups of the seasoned bread crumbs and the beaten eggs and mix well. Season to taste with salt and cayenne pepper. Use this mixture to stuff the eggplant shells. Top with the remaining bread crumbs. Bake at 350°F for 5-10 minutes, or until brown.

Left: Stuffed Eggplant with Shrimp – a mouthwatering seafood dish from bayou country.

The shrimp add a Louisiana flavor to these stuffed eggplants. You can also serve the filling in a casserole if you don't wish to stuff the eggplant shells.

JOHN D. FOLSE, LAFITTE'S LANDING,
P.O. BOX 1128, DONALDSONVILLE, LA

GREGORY'S GOLDEN PUFFS WITH NEW HAMPSHIRE SHRIMP MOUSSE

Choux pastry puffs make elegant hors d'oeuvres. Shape them small to serve with drinks, or larger for a first course. New Hampshire shrimp and Cheddar cheese make these especially good.

Preparation Time: 25 minutes
Cooking Time: 40 minutes
Oven Temperature: 420°F reduced to 250°F
Makes: about 24 puffs

INGREDIENTS

PUFFS
1 cup water
4oz butter
1 cup bread flour
5 eggs

MOUSSE
1lb fresh cooked New Hampshire shrimp
4oz New Hampshire Cheddar cheese
2 tbsps minced fresh garlic
6oz farm fresh sour cream
½ tsp salt
½ tsp white pepper
½ tsp dry vermouth
½ tsp Helmet mustard, ground
1oz Danish blue cheese

METHOD

To prepare the puffs, bring the water and butter to the boil in a heavy pan. Once boiling, sift in the cup of flour and stir over very low heat with a whisk. Once the mixture comes away from the sides of the pan, beat in the eggs, one at a time. Continue beating in the eggs over low heat until the mixture is smooth and shiny—it may not be necessary to add all the eggs. Transfer the pastry into a pastry bag fitted with a large plain tip. Pipe the mixture out onto a greased baking sheet in amounts about 2 inches tall and equally wide. Alternatively, pipe out in decorative shapes such as little turbans or simple round mounds. Place in a preheated oven for 30 minutes. Reduce the heat to 250°F for 10 minutes longer, or until the puffs are golden brown and crisp. Remove from the oven and, using a sharp skewer, pierce a hole the size of a small plain piping tip in the bottom. Allow to cool completely while preparing the mousse.

In a food processor, combine all the mousse ingredients and blend until smooth. When the puffs are completely cold, fill a pastry bag fitted with a plain tip with the mousse mixture and pipe through the prepared holes in the puffs. Do not fill the puffs more than 30 minutes before serving.

GREGORY MARTIN,
WHITE RABBIT CATERING,
HOOKSETT, NH

NEW ENGLAND CLAM CHOWDER

French fishermen invented this thick soup-stew, but New Englanders adopted it as their own, using the delicious varieties of clams found along their coastlines.

Preparation Time: 30 minutes
Cooking Time: 20 minutes
Serves: 6-8

INGREDIENTS

2lbs clams (1lb shelled or canned clams)
3oz rindless bacon, diced
2 medium onions, finely diced
1 tbsp flour
6 medium potatoes, peeled and cubed
Salt and pepper
4 cups milk
1 cup light cream
Chopped parsley (optional)

METHOD

Scrub the clams well and place them in a basin of cold water with a handful of flour to soak for 30 minutes. Drain the clams and place them in a deep saucepan with about ½ cup cold water. Cover and bring to the boil, stirring occasionally until all the shells open. Discard any shells that do not open. Strain the clam liquid and reserve it and set the clams aside to cool. Place the diced bacon in a large, deep saucepan and cook slowly until the fat is rendered. Turn up the heat and brown the bacon. Remove it to paper towel to drain. Add the onion to the bacon fat in the pan and cook slowly to soften. Stir in the flour and add the potatoes, salt, pepper, milk and reserved clam juice. Cover and bring to the boil and cook for about 10 minutes, or until the potatoes are nearly tender. Remove the clams from their shells and chop them if large. Add to the soup along with the cream and diced bacon. Cook a further 10 minutes, or until the potatoes and clams are tender. Add the chopped parsley, if desired, and serve immediately.

New Hampshire's landscape (facing page) provides a feast for the eye, while her cuisine satisfies the most discerning palates with appetizers such as Gregory's Golden Puffs with New Hampshire Shrimp Mousse.

Left: Maine's rugged coastline provides the ingredients for famed New England Clam Chowder.

SHE CRAB SOUP

A female crab, with roe intact, is needed for a truly authentic soup. However, exceptions can be made with results just as delicious.

Preparation Time: 35-40 minutes
Cooking Time: 25 minutes
Serves: 4

INGREDIENTS

1 large crab, cooked
3 tbsps butter or margarine
1 onion, very finely chopped
2 tbsps flour
4 cups milk
6 tbsps sherry
Pinch salt, white pepper and ground mace
½ cup heavy cream, whipped
Red caviar

METHOD

To dress the crab, take off all the legs and the large claws. Crack the large claws and legs and extract the meat. Turn the crab shell over and press up with thumbs to push out the underbody. Cut this piece in quarters and use a skewer to pick out the meat. Discard the stomach sac and the lungs (dead

She Crab Soup (top right) and Jellied Avocado Salad (right) reflect something of the elegance of Maryland (facing page), a state that combines the best of both Northern and Southern cooking.

man's fingers). Set the white meat aside with the claw meat. Using a teaspoon, scrape out the brown meat from inside the shell and reserve it. If the roe is present reserve that, too. Melt the butter or margarine in a medium saucepan and soften the onion for about 3 minutes. Do not allow to brown. Stir in the flour and milk. Bring to the boil and then immediately turn down the heat to simmer. Add the brown meat from the crab and cook gently for about 20 minutes. Add the sherry, salt, pepper, mace, white crab meat and roe. Cook a further 5 minutes. Top each serving with a spoonful of whipped cream and red caviar.

JELLIED AVOCADO SALAD

Salads set with gelatine are cooling treats in summer or perfect do-ahead dishes anytime.

Preparation Time: 25 minutes plus 2 hours to set
Serves: 4-6

INGREDIENTS

Juice of 1 small lemon
1½ tbsps unflavored gelatine
2 ripe avocados
3oz cream cheese or low fat soft cheese
½ cup sour cream or natural yogurt
2 tbsps mayonnaise
3 oranges, peeled and segmented
Flat Italian parsley or coriander to garnish

METHOD

Reserve about 2 tsps of the lemon juice. Pour the rest into a small dish, sprinkle the gelatine on top and allow to stand until spongy. Cut the avocados in half and twist to separate. Reserve half of one avocado with the stone attached and brush the cut surface with lemon juice, wrap in plastic wrap and keep in the refrigerator. Remove the stone from the other half and scrape the pulp from the three halves into a food processor. Add the cheese, sour cream or yogurt and mayonnaise and process until smooth. Melt the gelatine and add it to the avocado mixture with the machine running. Place a small disc of wax paper in custard cups, oil the sides of the cups and the paper and pour in the mixture. Tap the cups lightly on a flat surface to smooth the top and eliminate any air bubbles, cover with plastic wrap and chill until set. Loosen the set mixture carefully from the sides of the cups and invert each onto a serving plate to unmold. Peel and slice the remaining avocado half and use to decorate the plate along with the orange segments. Place parsley or coriander leaves on top of each avocado mold to serve.

SMOKED FISH SPREAD

Preparation Time: 15 minutes
Serves: 3-4

INGREDIENTS

1lb smoked marlin, or other smoked fish, flaked
1 tbsp fresh chives, chopped
1 tbsp minced celery
1 tbsp lemon juice
¼-½ cup mayonnaise
¼ tsp pepper
⅛ tsp salt

METHOD

A state of surprising contrasts, Virginia boasts the old-world elegance of Colonial Williamsburg (right) and the homely simplicity of dishes such as Virginia Peanut Soup (below).

Combine all the ingredients and mix well. Serve this irresistible spread on crackers. It goes down well with pre-dinner drinks.

CHEF HEINZ EBERHARD,
GOURMET GALLEY,
PALM BEACH, FL

VIRGINIA PEANUT SOUP

Peanuts, popular all over the South, make a velvety rich soup that is easily made from ordinary store cupboard ingredients.

Preparation Time: 15 minutes
Cooking Time: 15 minutes
Serves: 4

Facing page: Crab Smithfield.

INGREDIENTS

4 tbsps butter or margarine
2 tbsps flour
1 cup creamy peanut butter
¼ tsp celery seed
2½ cups chicken stock
½ cup dry sherry
½ cup coarsely chopped peanuts

METHOD

Melt the butter or margarine in a medium saucepan. Remove from the heat and stir in the flour. Add the peanut butter and celery seed. Gradually pour on the stock, stirring constantly. Return the pan to the heat and simmer gently for about 15 minutes. Do not allow to boil rapidly. Stir in the sherry and ladle into a tureen or individual bowls. Sprinkle with the chopped peanuts.

CRAB MEAT BALLS

Delicious as a first course or a cocktail snack, crab meat balls can be made ahead, then coated and fried at the last minute.

Preparation Time: 40-50 minutes
Cooking Time: 3 minutes
Serves: 6-8

Below: Crab Meat Balls.

INGREDIENTS

1lb fresh or frozen crab meat, chopped finely
4 slices white bread, crusts removed and made into crumbs
1 tbsp butter or margarine
1 tbsp flour
½ cup milk
½ red or green chili, seeded and finely chopped
1 green onion, finely chopped
1 tbsp chopped parsley
Salt
Flour
2 eggs, beaten
Dry breadcrumbs
Oil for frying

METHOD

Combine the crab meat with the fresh breadcrumbs and set aside. Melt the butter and add the flour off the heat. Stir in the milk and return to moderate heat. Bring to the boil, stirring constantly. Stir the white sauce into the crab meat and bread-crumbs, adding the chili, onion and parsley. Season with salt to taste, cover and allow to cool completely. Shape the cold mixture into 1 inch balls with floured hands. Coat with beaten egg using a fork to turn balls in the mixture or use a pastry brush to coat with egg. Coat with the dry breadcrumbs. Fry in oil in a deep sauté pan, saucepan or deep-fat fryer at 350°F until golden brown and crisp, about 3 minutes per batch of 6. Turn occasionally while frying. Drain on paper towels and sprinkle lightly with salt.

CRAB SMITHFIELD

Virginia's famous Smithfield ham makes a wonderful addition to fresh crab meat in this quickly-made first course.

Preparation Time: 15 minutes
Cooking Time: 3 minutes
Serves: 2-4

INGREDIENTS

5oz crab meat
1oz Smithfield ham, cut into julienne slices
1oz butter

GARNISH

Parsley sprigs
Lemon wedges

METHOD

Melt the butter in a sauté pan. Add the crab meat and sauté for 2 minutes. Arrange the julienned ham on top and brown under the broiler for 1 minute. Garnish with sprigs of parsley and a lemon wedge before serving.

BRICE AND SHIRLEY PHILLIPS,
PHILLIPS WATERSIDE, NORFOLK, VA

AUTUMN BISQUE

Butternut squash and apples are at their best in the fall. They were both staple foods grown by the settlers for their keeping qualities. They complement one another well and taste delicious in a smooth, creamy soup.

Preparation Time: 25 minutes

Facing page: the Atlantic shoreline at Cape May. Lying at the southern tip of New Jersey, the city claims to be one of the nation's oldest beach resorts. Delicious fresh seafood complements the region's other varied attractions.

Cooking Time: 40-50 minutes
Serves: 4-6

INGREDIENTS

*1 small butternut squash, unpeeled, halved and seeded
(approximately 1lb in weight)
2 green apples, peeled, cored and chopped
1 medium onion, peeled and chopped
Pinch rosemary
Pinch marjoram
1 quart chicken stock
2 slices white bread, trimmed and cubed
1½ tsps salt
¼ tsp pepper
2 egg yolks
¼ cup heavy cream*

METHOD

Combine the squash, apples, onion, herbs, stock, bread cubes, salt and pepper in a heavy saucepan. Bring to the boil and simmer, uncovered, for 30-45 minutes. Take out the squash with a draining spoon and scoop out the flesh, discarding the skins. Return the pulp to the soup. Purée the soup in a blender or food processor until smooth and return to the rinsed out saucepan. In a small bowl, beat the egg yolks and cream together. Beat in a little of the hot soup and then stir back into the saucepan with the rest of the soup. Cook gently, stirring constantly until thickened. Do not allow the soup to boil or the eggs will curdle. Serve immediately.

Below: Sea Island Shrimp.

SEA ISLAND SHRIMP

Although this is a recipe from the Carolinas, it is popular everywhere succulent shrimp are available.

Preparation Time: 30 minutes
Cooking Time: 15 minutes
Serves: 2-4

INGREDIENTS

*2 dozen raw large shrimp, unpeeled
4 tbsps butter or margarine
1 small red pepper, seeded and finely chopped
2 green onions, finely chopped
½ tsp dry mustard
2 tsps dry sherry
1 tsp Worcester sauce
4oz cooked crab meat
6 tbsps fresh breadcrumbs
1 tbsp chopped parsley
2 tbsps mayonnaise
Salt and pepper
1 small egg, beaten
Grated Parmesan cheese
Paprika*

METHOD

Remove all of the shrimp shells except for the very tail ends. Remove the black veins on the rounded sides. Cut the shrimp down the length of the curved side and press each one open. Melt half of the butter or margarine in a small pan and cook the pepper to soften, about 3 minutes. Add the green onions and cook a further 2 minutes. Combine the peppers with the mustard, sherry, Worcester sauce, crab meat, bread-crumbs, parsley and mayonnaise. Add seasoning and enough egg to bind together. Spoon the stuffing onto the shrimp and sprinkle with the Parmesan cheese and paprika. Melt the remaining butter or margarine and drizzle over the shrimp. Bake in a pre-heated 350°F oven for about 10 minutes. Serve immediately.

STUFFED QUAHOGS

Quahogs are hard-shell clams that are used for chowder when large, and eaten on the half shell when smaller. To facilitate opening, place well-scrubbed clams in a pan in a moderate oven and heat until they open. Use a strong knife to pry off the top shells. One or two stuffed clams make an excellent hors d'oeuvre or appetizer, more make a great snack or meal. One clam stuffs one shell.

Preparation Time: 20 minutes
Cooking Time: 15 minutes
Oven Temperature: 375°F
Serves: 4

INGREDIENTS

*8 quahogs, shelled, poached 3 minutes and chopped
1 onion, chopped
¼ tsp oregano
1 green and 1 red pepper, chopped
1 clove garlic, crushed
3 tbsps butter
Fresh bread crumbs
Grated Romano or Parmesan cheese*

METHOD

Sautée the onions and peppers in butter until glassy, add the chopped garlic and cook another 1-2 minutes over low heat. Stir in the chopped clams and an equal amount of fresh bread crumbs. Add about ½ tsp grated cheese per clam. Moisten with additional melted butter and/or clam juice. Stuff into each clam shell half and bake until hot and slightly browned. Serve accompanied with lemon wedges and hot pepper sauce (Tabasco).

THE OLYMPIA TEA ROOM,
BAY STREET, WATCH HILL, RI

Right: Meeting Street
Crab Meat.

MEETING STREET CRAB MEAT

This tasty seafood dish may also be made with shrimp. Use 1½lbs raw, peeled shrimp in place of the crab meat.

Preparation Time: 20 minutes
Cooking Time: 15 minutes
Serves: 4

INGREDIENTS

4 tbsps butter
4 tbsps flour
1 cup cream
4 tbsps sherry
Salt and pepper to taste
1lb white crab meat
¾ cup grated sharp cheese

METHOD

In a saucepan, melt the butter. Gradually stir in the flour to make a smooth paste. Cook for a few minutes over a low heat then gradually stir in the cream. Add the sherry, salt and pepper. Cook over a medium heat, stirring often, until the sauce is thickened. Remove from the heat and stir in the crab meat. Pour the mixture into a buttered casserole, or into 4 individual baking dishes. Sprinkle with the grated cheese and bake at 400°F for approximately 10 minutes, or until the cheese melts. Be careful not to overcook.

MRS. THOMAS A. HUGUENIN,
CHARLESTON, SC
(FROM "CHARLESTON RECEIPTS,"
COMPILED AND EDITED BY THE JUNIOR
LEAGUE OF CHARLESTON, INC.)

HARVEST VEGETABLE SOUP

Preparation Time: 25 minutes
Cooking Time: 22 minutes
Serves: 8

INGREDIENTS

3 cups strong veal stock
3 cups strong chicken stock
½ tsp basil leaves
½ tsp thyme leaves
1 bay leaf
¼ tsp minced garlic
¼ cup diced mushrooms

¼ cup clean chopped spinach
2 tbsps tomato paste
¼ cup diced zucchini
¼ cup diced summer squash
½ cup diced onions
¼ cup diced carrots
¼ cup diced celery
¼ cup broccoli flowerets
¼ cup diced cabbage
¼ cup diced cauliflower flowerets
3 tbsps butter

METHOD

In a large stock pot, melt the butter and add the herbs, garlic, celery and carrots. Stir well and cook until the vegetables are beginning to soften but not browning. Add the onion, broccoli and cauliflower. Stir well and cook for 2 minutes. Add the zucchini, summer squash and mushrooms and cook for a further 2 minutes. Add the spinach and cabbage and mix well. Pour in the veal stock and chicken stock and add the tomato paste. Bring to the boil and stir occasionally. Reduce the heat and let the soup simmer for 20 minutes. Remove from the heat and add salt and pepper to taste. Let the soup cool to room temperature, cover and refrigerate overnight. The fat will rise to the surface and solidify, making it easy to remove. Spoon off the hardened fat and bring the soup back to the boil. Use your favorite garnish, such as grated cheese, croûtons, or chopped parsley. Reheating and serving the soup the next day gives the flavors a chance to meld together.

CHEF JAMES E. LOWE,
THE VILLAGE INN,
LENOX, MA

CRAB MEAT IMPERIAL

Another of New Orleans' famous dishes, this makes a delicious warm weather salad for lunches, light suppers or elegant appetizers.

Preparation Time: 45 minutes
Cooking Time: 10 minutes
Serves: 2-4

INGREDIENTS

2 small crabs, boiled
2 tbsps oil
4 green onions
1 small green pepper, seeded and finely chopped
1 stick celery, finely chopped
1 clove garlic, crushed
¾ cup prepared mayonnaise
1 tbsp mild mustard
Dash tabasco and Worcestershire sauce
1 piece canned pimento, drained and finely chopped
2 tbsps chopped parsley
Salt and pepper
Lettuce, curly endive or raddichio (optional)

METHOD

To shell the crabs, first remove all the legs and the large claws by twisting and pulling them away from the body. Turn the shell over and, using your thumbs, push the body away from the flat shell. Set the body aside. Remove the stomach sack and the lungs or dead man's fingers and discard them. Using a small teaspoon, scrape the brown body meat out of the flat

Right: Crab Meat
Imperial.

shell. Using a sharp knife, cut the body of the crab in four pieces and, using a pick or a skewer, push out all the meat. Crack the large claws and remove the meat in one piece if possible. Crack the legs and remove the meat as well, leaving the small, thin legs in the shell. Set all the meat aside. Scrub the shells if desired to use for serving. Heat the oil in a small sauté pan or frying pan. Chop the white parts of the green onions and add to the oil with the green pepper, celery and garlic. Sauté over gentle heat for about 10 minutes, stirring often to soften the vegetables but not brown them. Remove from the heat and set aside. When cool, add the mayonnaise, mustard, tabasco, Worcestershire sauce, pimento and finely chopped tops of the green onions. Spoon the reserved brown body meat from the crabs back into each shell or serving dish. Mix the remaining crab meat with the dressing, reserving the crab claws for garnish, if desired. They may also be shredded and added to the other crab meat. Do not overmix the sauce as the crab meat should stay in large pieces. Spoon into the shells on top of the brown body meat, sprinkle with chopped parsley and place the crab shells on serving plates, surrounding them with lettuce leaves, if desired. Garnish with the shelled crab claws and use the crab legs if desired. Sprinkle with parsley and serve immediately.

CHALUPAS

These are tortillas in another form, this time a snack with spicy meat. Create your own combination with a selection of different toppings.

Preparation Time: 40 minutes
Cooking Time: 30 minutes
Makes: 10

INGREDIENTS

Half quantity Tortilla recipe
Oil for frying
Full quantity Red Sauce
(see recipe for Southwestern Stir-fry)
12oz ground beef
2 cloves garlic, crushed
1 tsp dried oregano
2 tsps cumin
Salt and pepper
3oz frozen corn
4 tbsps raisins

TOPPINGS

6-8 chopped green onions
4-6 diced tomatoes
Half a small head lettuce, shredded
½ cup sour cream
1 cup shredded cheese

METHOD

Prepare the tortillas according to the recipe and divide the dough in 10. After the required resting time, roll the balls of dough into 3½ inch rounds. Prepare the Red Sauce according to the recipe instructions and set it aside. Heat at least 2 inches of oil in a frying pan, sauté pan or medium saucepan. When hot, place in one tortilla and fry briefly until just crisp. Drain and keep them warm. Cook the beef slowly until the fat begins to render. Add the garlic, oregano and cumin and raise the heat to brown the meat. Season to taste and then stir in enough of the Red Sauce to moisten the meat well. Add the corn and raisins, cover the pan and leave to stand for 5 minutes. Spoon the meat onto the tortillas and drizzle over more sauce. Garnish with your choice of toppings.

CATFISH HORS D'OEUVRE

These well spiced and crispy morsels are a favorite in the Governor's Mansion.

Preparation Time: 20 minutes
Cooking Time: 10−15 minutes
Serves: 4−8

INGREDIENTS

4 catfish fillets, diced
1 cup yellow cornmeal
½ tsp garlic salt
½ tsp cayenne
Oil for deep fat frying

METHOD

Combine the cornmeal, garlic salt and cayenne pepper. Roll the diced catfish in this mixture to coat. Deep fry in fat which has been heated to 375°F, or until a 1-inch cube of bread browns in 1 minute. The fish pieces will sink to the bottom of the pan. When they rise to the surface they are done. The pieces should be golden brown. Drain on paper towels and serve hot.

LIZA, GOVERNOR'S MANSION,
LITTLE ROCK, AR

SHRIMP AND MUSHROOM SALAD

This original salad makes use of some of Florida's most delicious seafood.

Preparation Time: 30 minutes
Cooking Time: 1 minute
Serves: 8

INGREDIENTS

2lbs cooked shrimp
½lb snow peas, topped and tailed
1lb very white mushrooms, sliced
1 cup toasted pecans
2 heads Boston or bibb lettuce

VINAIGRETTE

1 tbsp Dijon-style mustard
1 clove garlic, minced
4 tbsps cider vinegar
Dash lime juice
1 cup salad oil
Salt and pepper to taste

METHOD

Peel and devein the shrimp. Blanch the snow peas in the boiling salted water for 45 seconds, then drain. Toss together

Facing page: Catfish Hors d'Oeuvre is a favorite appetizer in the Arkansas Governor's Mansion at Little Rock (below).

Facing page: Shrimp Bisque, a classic Cajun recipe from Louisiana.

the mushrooms, shrimp, snow peas and pecans. To prepare the vinaigrette, place the mustard, garlic, lime juice and vinegar in the bowl of a food processor. Pulse a few times, then run continuously while adding the oil in a slow stream. Season with salt and pepper to taste. To serve, toss the salad in the vinaigrette. Line salad plates with the lettuce and arrange the salad on top.

ART SMITH, GOVERNOR'S MANSION, TALLAHASSEE, FL

SHRIMP BISQUE

This classic Cajun recipe makes a first course or a full meal. It isn't a smooth purée like its French counterpart.

Preparation Time: 20 minutes
Cooking Time: 8-10 minutes
Serves: 6

INGREDIENTS

3 tbsps butter or margarine
1 onion, finely chopped
1 red pepper, seeded and finely chopped
2 sticks celery, finely chopped
1 clove garlic, minced
Pinch dry mustard and cayenne pepper
2 tsps paprika
3 tbsps flour
4 cups fish stock
1 sprig thyme and bay leaf
8oz raw, peeled shrimp
Salt and pepper
Snipped chives

METHOD

Melt the butter or margarine and add the onion, pepper, celery and garlic. Cook gently to soften. Stir in the mustard, cayenne, paprika and flour. Cook about 3 minutes over gentle heat, stirring occasionally. Pour on the stock gradually, stirring until well blended. Add the thyme and bay leaf and bring to the boil. Reduce the heat and simmer about 5 minutes or until thickened, stirring occasionally. Add the shrimp and cook until pink and curled, about 5 minutes. Season with salt and pepper to taste and top with snipped chives before serving.

CREAM OF TOMATO AND CHEDDAR SOUP

Tomato soup used to be one of the more fashionable soups for a company dinner. Cheddar cheese used to be made in every state where there was a dairy industry and was a popular food across the country. With tomatoes and cheese being such a good combination, it was natural to bring them together in one delicious soup.

Preparation Time: 25 minutes
Cooking Time: 1 hour 10 minutes
Serves: 12

INGREDIENTS

1 small onion, chopped
4 stalks celery, leaves removed
3 carrots, peeled
2lbs canned Italian plum tomatoes
3 tbsps whole mixed pickling spice tied in a small cheesecloth bag

Below: Cream of Tomato and Cheddar Soup – a delicious combination of two simple ingredients.

4 tbsps extra virgin olive oil
1 tsp Worcestershire sauce
¼ tsp Tabasco
2 quarts veal stock
¾-1lb Vermont Cheddar cheese double aged (4 years)
if possible, and shredded
5oz butter
5oz flour
8oz butter
1 cup heavy cream
Salt and black pepper to taste

METHOD

Chop the onions, celery and carrots finely. Sauté in the olive oil in a 1 gallon soup pot until slightly softened. Add the tomatoes, bag of spices, Worcestershire sauce and Tabasco and simmer for 1 hour, stirring often. Remove the spice bag and purée mixture in a food processor or food mill until smooth. Return to the rinsed out pan, add the veal stock and return the spice bag to the soup. Bring to the boil, reduce the heat and simmer until reduced by about a quarter. Put 5oz butter in a small saucepan and stir in the flour. Cook over low heat for 5 minutes, but do not brown. Gradually beat the roux into the soup and bring to the boil. Simmer for 10 minutes, add Cheddar cheese, remaining butter and cream. Adjust the seasonings and serve immediately. Garnish with crôutons, additional Cheddar cheese or chopped parsley, if desired.

CHEF STEPHEN MONGEON,
THE RED LION INN, STOCKBRIDGE, MA

A GREEN-PEAS SOUP

This is a summery version of a hearty winter staple. Green peas and mint add a freshness and a light, delicate taste to dried split peas.

Preparation Time: 30 minutes
Cooking Time: 45-50 minutes
Serves: 8-10

INGREDIENTS

¾ cup dried split peas
1¼lbs frozen peas
3oz fresh mint leaves
½ cup butter or margarine, melted
Pinch salt and pepper
Sprigs of fresh mint to garnish

METHOD

Place the split peas with about 6 cups water in a heavy saucepan. Cover, bring to the boil and cook until very tender, about 40 minutes. Strain the peas and reserve the liquid. Pour the liquid back into the saucepan and add the frozen peas. Chop the mint leaves, reserving some for garnish, and add to the peas. Bring to the boil in a covered saucepan. Meanwhile, add the melted butter to the dried peas and push through a strainer or work in a food processor to form a smooth purée. Add the purée to the green peas, mixing well. Add salt and pepper to taste. Pour the hot soup into a tureen and garnish with sprigs or leaves of mint. Serve immediately.

SCALLOP AND AVOCADO SEVICHE

The scallops in this recipe "cook" in the refrigerator! This dish is simple to prepare and makes a delicious first course. It will keep for 1 week in the refrigerator if stirred daily.

Left: farm buildings at Old Chippewa City, north of Chippewa Falls, Wisconsin. Founded as a lumbering town, it is now the center of the region's dairy and agricultural activity.

Facing page: the New York State Capitol at Albany.

Right: Scallop and Avocado Seviche – "cook" it in the refrigerator for a simple but delicious first course!

Preparation Time: 20 minutes plus 36-48 hours in the refrigerator
Serves: 6

INGREDIENTS

2lbs scallops, sliced
Juice of 5 limes
1 cup salad oil
2 tomatoes, peeled, seeded and diced
2 green peppers, diced
1 avocado, diced
½ Spanish onion, minced
2 cloves garlic, crushed
¾ tsp cayenne pepper
1 tbsp white vinegar
1 tsp salt

METHOD

Combine all the ingredients and refrigerate. Cover the bowl and allow to marinate 36-48 hours, or until the scallops are opaque all the way through. Stir the seviche daily. Serve on lettuce leaves on individual plates.

NEAL SOLOMON, EXECUTIVE CHEF, HAMPSHIRE HOUSE, BEACON STREET, BOSTON, MA

INDIAN BREAD WITH CHORIZO AND SALSA

A version of this bread recipe has been baked by American Indians for hundreds of years. It's delicious served plain, too.

Preparation Time: 45 minutes−1 hour
Cooking Time: 1-2 minutes per piece.
Chorizo topping: 25 minutes for the potatoes and sausages
Serves: 4-6

INGREDIENTS

BREAD
2 cups all-purpose flour
1 tbsp baking powder
Pinch salt
1 tbsp vegetable shortening
2 tsps cumin seed
¾ cup plus 2 tbsps water
CHORIZO TOPPING
1lb chorizo sausage
2 medium red potatoes, scrubbed
4 green onions, chopped

SALSA

1 clove garlic
1oz coriander leaves
1 tsp fresh oregano
Half or less fresh red or green chili, seeded
Pinch salt and dry mustard
Juice of 2 limes
¾ cup oil
Shredded lettuce, crumbled goat's milk cheese and chopped tomatoes to garnish

METHOD

Sift the flour, baking powder and salt into a bowl. Rub in the shortening until the mixture resembles coarse crumbs and then stir in the cumin seed. Stir in enough water to make a soft, slightly sticky dough. Knead several times, cover and leave to stand for 15-20 minutes. Divide the dough into 8 pieces and roll or pat into 5 inch circles on a well-floured surface. Make a hole in the center of each with your finger and leave the circles to stand, covered, for 30 minutes. Meanwhile, boil the potatoes in their skins in a covered saucepan. Place the chorizo in a sauté pan and cover with water. Cover the pan and bring to the boil. Lower the heat and simmer about 10 minutes, or until just tender. Remove the chorizo from the water and peel off the casings while the sausage is still warm. Chop sausage roughly and set aside. When the potatoes are tender, drain them and leave to cool. Cut the potatoes into ½ inch dice. Place the garlic, coriander, oregano, chili, salt and mustard into a food processor and add the lime juice. Process until well blended. With the machine running, pour the oil through the funnel in a thin, steady stream. Process until smooth and adjust the seasoning. Pour the oil for cooking the bread into a deep-fat fryer, large saucepan or deep sauté pan to a depth of about 2-3 inches. Heat to 375°F. Carefully lower in one dough circle and push it underneath the oil with a large metal spoon. Fry for about 30 seconds, turn over and fry the other side. Drain each while frying the others. Mix the chorizo, green onions and potatoes with enough of the salsa to moisten. Arrange the shredded lettuce on top of the bread and spoon on the chorizo topping. Spoon on any remaining salsa, sprinkle with chopped tomato and crumbled cheese.

OREGANO OYSTERS

The combination of oregano and the anise taste of Pernod is an unusual but very complementary one, especially with fresh oysters.

Preparation Time: 25 minutes
Cooking Time: 20-25 minutes
Serves: 4

INGREDIENTS

1 tbsp butter or margarine
1 clove garlic, crushed
1 tbsp chopped parsley
1 tbsp chopped fresh oregano or 1½ tsps dried oregano
1 tbsp Pernod
¾ cup heavy cream
Salt and pepper
24 oysters on the half shell
12 strips bacon, cooked and crumbled
Coarse salt

METHOD

Melt the butter or margarine in a saucepan. Add the garlic and cook to soften, but do not brown. Add the parsley, oregano, Pernod and cream. Bring to the boil and lower the heat to simmering. Strain on any liquid from the oysters and then loosen them from their shells with a small, sharp knife. Cook the mixture until reduced by about one quarter and slightly thickened. Test the seasoning and set the mixture aside. Pour about 1 inch coarse salt into a baking pan. Place the oysters on top of the salt and twist the shells into the salt so that they stand level. Spoon some of the cream over each oyster and sprinkle with the crumbled bacon. Bake in a pre-heated 400°F oven for 15-18 minutes. Serve immediately.

AVOCADO SOUP

Avocados feature frequently in California cooking. A cold soup like this makes an easy summer meal.

Preparation Time: 20-25 minutes plus 2 hours chilling in the refrigerator
Serves 4:

INGREDIENTS

2 large ripe avocados
1½ cups natural yogurt
2 cups chicken or vegetable stock
½ clove garlic, minced
Juice of 1 lemon
2 tsps chopped fresh oregano
Salt and white pepper
Chopped parsley to garnish

Facing page: Oregano Oysters – a taste of the South with the distinctive flavor of Pernod.

Avocados are a common ingredient in California cooking, and nowhere are they used to better effect than in tasty Avocado Soup (below).

METHOD

Cut the avocados in half lengthwise and twist to separate. Tap the stone sharply with a knife and twist to remove. Place the avocado halves cut side down on a flat surface. Score the skin with a sharp knife and then peel the strips of skin backwards to remove them. Cut the avocado into pieces and place in a food processor. Reserve 4 tbsps yogurt and add the remaining yogurt and other ingredients, except the parsley, to the avocado. Process until smooth and chill thoroughly. Pour the soup into bowls or a tureen and garnish with reserved yogurt. Sprinkle with parsley and serve chilled.

CABBAGE SOUP

An unusual combination, but one that uses everyday ingredients, readily available and simple to prepare. A pressure cooker will cut the cooking time by a third. This soup tastes even better when reheated the next day.

Preparation Time: 25 minutes plus overnight soaking
Cooking Time: 1 hour 50 minutes
Serves: 4-6

INGREDIENTS

2 cups dried kidney beans
3 tbsps duck or goose fat or butter
1 medium onion, thinly sliced
1 small cabbage, thinly sliced
4 cloves garlic, chopped
2 tomatoes, peeled, seeded and chopped

METHOD

Pick over and rinse the beans. Soak overnight in 2 quarts of cold water. In a heavy based pot, melt the fat or butter and cook the onion and cabbage slowly, stirring occasionally until translucent. Add the remaining ingredients, including the beans and soaking water. Bring to the boil and then simmer for 1½ hours or until the beans are tender. Check the seasoning and serve.

NEW ENGLAND CULINARY INSTITUTE,
MONTPELIER, VT

BUTTERNUT SQUASH SOUP

Preparation Time: 25 minutes
Cooking Time: 30-45 minutes
Serves: 4-6

INGREDIENTS

1 butternut squash, peeled, seeds removed and cubed
1 onion, diced
1 apple, peeled, cored and sliced
2 chicken bouillon cubes
1½ cups milk
2 tbsps brown sugar
Pinch salt and pepper
2 tbsps butter

METHOD

Place the prepared squash in a large pot with the apple and half the onion. Pour in the bouillon, cover the pot and cook until the squash is just tender. Do not overcook. Melt the butter

Right: the monumental landscape of Zion National Park, Utah.

OYSTERS CASINO

DANIEL ROUTHIER,
DEAN'S MILL FARM,
STONINGTON, CT

These tasty oysters make a delightful first course.

Preparation Time: 15 minutes
Cooking Time: 6-8 minutes
Serves: 3-4

INGREDIENTS

12 oysters
½ small green pepper, diced
½ small onion, diced
1 pinch seafood seasoning per oyster
½ cup Monterey Jack cheese, grated
3 strips bacon, cut into 1-inch pieces
2 drops lemon juice per oyster

TO SERVE

Drawn butter
Lemon wedges

METHOD

Clean the oysters and loosen from the shells at the muscle. Place a little finely diced green pepper and onion on top of each and sprinkle with the seafood seasoning and lemon juice. Cover each oyster with grated Monterey Jack cheese and top with a piece of bacon. Bake at 350°F for 6-8 minutes. Serve with drawn butter and lemon wedges.

BRICE AND SHIRLEY PHILLIPS,
PHILLIPS WATERSIDE, NORFOLK, VA

CORN AND POTATO CHOWDER

Such a filling soup, this is really a complete meal in a bowl. Corn is a favorite ingredient in Southern cooking.

Preparation Time: 25 minutes
Cooking Time: 25-30 minutes
Serves: 4-6

INGREDIENTS

6 medium potatoes, peeled
Chicken or vegetable stock
1 onion, finely chopped
2 tbsps butter or margarine
1 tbsp flour
4oz cooked ham, chopped
4 ears fresh corn or about 4oz canned or frozen corn
3 cups milk
Salt and dash tabasco
Finely chopped parsley

METHOD

Quarter the potatoes and place them in a deep saucepan. Add stock to cover and the onion, and bring the mixture to the boil. Lower the heat and simmer, partially covered, until the potatoes are soft, about 15-20 minutes. Drain the potatoes, reserving ¾ pint of the cooking liquid. Mash the potatoes and combine with reserved liquid. Melt the butter or margarine in a clean pan, add the ham and cook briefly. Stir in the flour and pour over the potato mixture, mixing well. If using fresh corn, remove the husks and silk and, holding one end of the corn, stand the ear upright. Use a large, sharp knife and cut against the cob vertically from top to bottom just scraping off the kernels. Add the corn and milk to the potato mixture and bring almost to the boil. Do not boil the corn rapidly as this will toughen it. Add a pinch of salt and a dash of tabasco, and garnish with parsley before serving.

CIOPPINO

California's famous and delicious fish stew is Italian in heritage, but a close relative of French Bouillabaise, too.

Preparation Time: 40 minutes
Cooking Time: 40 minutes
Serves: 6-8

INGREDIENTS

1lb spinach, well washed
1 tbsp each chopped fresh basil, thyme, rosemary, and sage
2 tbsps chopped fresh marjoram
4 tbsps chopped parsley

1 large red pepper, seeded and finely chopped
2 cloves garlic, crushed
24 large fresh clams or 48 mussels, well scrubbed
1 large crab, cracked
1lb monkfish or rock salmon (huss)
12 large shrimp, cooked and unpeeled
1lb canned plum tomatoes and juice
2 tbsps tomato paste
4 tbsps olive oil
Pinch salt and pepper
½-1 cup dry white wine
Water

METHOD

Chop the spinach leaves roughly after removing any tough stems. Combine the spinach with the herbs, chopped red pepper and garlic, and set aside. Discard any clams or mussels with broken shells or ones that do not close when tapped. Place the shellfish in the bottom of a large pot and sprinkle over a layer of the spinach mixture. Prepare the crab as for Crab Louis, leaving the shells on the claws after cracking them slightly. Place the crab on top of the spinach and then add another spinach layer. Add the fish and a spinach layer, followed by the shrimp and any remaining spinach. Mix the tomatoes, tomato paste, oil, wine and seasonings and pour over the seafood and spinach. Cover the pot and simmer the mixture for about 40 minutes. If more liquid is necessary, add water. Spoon into soup bowls, dividing the fish and shell fish evenly.

JEKYLL ISLAND SHRIMP

Named for an island off the Georgia coast, this make a rich appetizer or an elegant main course.

Preparation Time: 35-40 minutes
Cooking Time: 20 minutes
Serves: 2-4

INGREDIENTS

2lbs cooked shrimp
4 tbsps butter, softened
Pinch salt, white pepper and cayenne
1 clove garlic, crushed
6 tbsps fine dry breadcrumbs
2 tbsps chopped parsley
4 tbsps sherry
Lemon wedges or slices

METHOD

To prepare the shrimp, remove the heads and legs first. Peel off the shells, carefully removing the tail shells. Remove the black vein running down the length of the rounded side with a wooden pick. Arrange shrimp in a shallow casserole or individual dishes. Combine the remaining ingredients, except the lemon garnish, mixing well. Spread the mixture to completely cover the shrimp and place in a pre-heated 375°F oven for about 20 minutes, or until the butter melts and the crumbs become crisp. Garnish with lemon wedges or slices.

Facing page: Cioppino. Both Italian and French in origin, this dish reflects something of California's cosmopolitan character.

Left: Jekyll Island Shrimp. Mouthwatering in any dish, shrimp really come into their own in this Georgia specialty.

America Cooks

CHAPTER

2

FISH AND SEAFOOD

Previous pages: Florida
Lobster Medallions form
part of a spectacular
seafood arrangement.

FLORIDA LOBSTER MEDALLIONS

The lobster medallions make a spectacular centerpiece to the
Gourmet Galley Raw Bar.

Preparation Time: 45 minutes
Cooking Time: 10 minutes
Serves: 4 as an appetizer

INGREDIENTS

1 whole lobster
½lb cream cheese, softened

GARNISH

Black olives, sliced
Fresh parsley

METHOD

Place the whole lobster in salted water to cover and bring to
the boil. Boil for approximately 5 minutes, or until the lobster
turns bright red. Cool, then slit the underside of the tail.
Remove the meat, being careful not to cut through the hard
top shell. Cut the meat into large, bite-size morsels. Attach
the morsels in rows to the top of the lobster shell using the
softened cream cheese. Garnish with slices of black olives
and parsley.

CHEF HEINZ EBERHARD,
GOURMET GALLEY,
PALM BEACH, FL

Right: Truite au Bleu – a
delicious recipe for this
delicately flavored fish.

TRUITE AU BLEU

The French influence is at work in this recipe. It is, of course,
only the skin of the trout which turns blue when cooked
by this method. Success depends on using very fresh fish
and minimal handling to preserve the natural slime on the
fish skin.

Preparation Time: 30 minutes
Cooking Time: 40 minutes
Serves: 4

INGREDIENTS

4 live trout
24 live crawfish
⅓ cup red wine vinegar
1 small onion, peeled and sliced
1 small carrot, peeled and sliced
½ a lemon, sliced
2 sprigs fresh thyme
2 tsps salt
Melted butter for serving

METHOD

Combine all the ingredients except the fish and melted butter
in a large pot and add 1 quart of water to make a court bouillon.
Simmer for 30 minutes and allow to cool. Kill the trout by
hitting it on the head once sharply with a heavy object. With
a sharp knife, eviscerate the fish. Place the trout and crawfish
into the court bouillon. Bring back to the boil and allow to
simmer. Turn off the heat and let stand 10 minutes before
removing the trout and crawfish to a heated platter for serving.
Serve with melted butter.

NEW ENGLAND CULINARY INSTITUTE,
MONTPELIER, VT

Facing page: appealing in taste as well as appearance, China Beach Salad reflects something of the Chinese influence in California cooking.

CRAB LOUIS

This salad is legendary on Fisherman's Wharf in San Francisco. Once tasted, it is sure to become a favorite.

Preparation Time: 30-40 minutes
Serves: 4

INGREDIENTS

2 large cooked crabs
1 head iceberg lettuce
4 large tomatoes
4 hard-boiled eggs
16 black olives
1 cup prepared mayonnaise
4 tbsps whipping cream
4 tbsps chili sauce or tomato chutney
½ green pepper, seeded and finely diced
3 green onions, finely chopped
Salt and pepper

METHOD

To prepare the crabs, break off the claws and set them aside. Turn the crabs over and press up with thumbs to separate the body from the shell of each. Cut the body into quarters and use a skewer to pick out the white meat. Discard the stomach sac and the lungs (dead-man's fingers). Scrape out the brown meat from the shell to use, if desired. Crack the large claws and legs and remove the meat. Break into shreds, discarding any shell or cartilage. Combine all the meat and set it aside.

Shred the lettuce finely, quarter the tomatoes and chop the eggs. Combine the mayonnaise, cream, chili sauce or chutney, green pepper and green onions and mix well. Arrange the shredded lettuce on serving plates and divide the crab meat evenly. Spoon some of the dressing over each serving of crab and sprinkle with the chopped egg. Garnish each serving with tomato wedges and olives and serve the remaining dressings separately.

CHINA BEACH SALAD

Named for a stretch of beach near San Francisco, this recipe reflects the Chinese heritage in California's past and its present passion for salads.

Preparation Time: 30 minutes
Serves: 4-6

INGREDIENTS

1lb cooked, peeled shrimp
1lb seedless white grapes, halved if large
6 sticks celery, thinly sliced on diagonal
4oz toasted flaked almonds
4oz canned water chestnuts, sliced or diced
8oz canned lichees or 12oz fresh litchis, peeled
1 small fresh pineapple, peeled, cored
and cut into pieces
1½ cups mayonnaise

Right: Crab Louis, a West Coast specialty that has achieved international fame.

1 tbsp honey
1 tbsp light soy sauce
2 tbps mild curry powder
Juice of half a lime
Chinese cabbage or Belgian endive (chicory)

METHOD

Combine the shrimp, grapes, celery, almonds, water chestnuts and litchis in a large bowl. Trim off the top and bottom of the pineapple and quarter. Slice off the points of each quarter to remove the core. Slice the pineapple skin away and cut the flesh into bite-size pieces. Add to the shrimp and toss to mix. Break the Chinese cabbage or endive and wash them well. If using Chinese cabbage, shred the leafy part finely, saving the thicker ends of the leaves for other use. Place the Chinese cabbage on salad plates. Mix the remaining dressing ingredients thoroughly. Pile the salad ingredients onto the leaves and spoon over some of the dressing, leaving the ingredients showing. Separate chicory leaves and arrange them whole. Serve remaining dressing separately.

SALMON AMANDINE

Preparation Time: 25 minutes
Cooking Time: 50 minutes
Oven Temperature: 350°F
Serves: 8

INGREDIENTS

5-6lb whole dressed salmon

STUFFING

6 cups crushed Ritz crackers
5 tbsps melted butter
¾ cup cream sherry
2 tsps salt
2 tsps Worcestershire sauce
2 drops red pepper sauce
1½lbs Maine crab meat

COURT BOUILLON

4 cups water
3 celery sticks, diced
1 quartered onion, stuck with whole cloves

GARNISH

1lb blanched, sliced almonds
1 egg white

METHOD

Remove the backbone from the salmon and combine with the court bouillon ingredients in a saucepan or a fish steamer. Bring to the boil and allow to simmer while preparing the stuffing. Combine all the stuffing ingredients and mix well. Spoon the stuffing into the cavity of the salmon. Rub the fish with melted butter and place in the top of the fish steamer or into a roasting pan. If using a roasting pan, carefully pour the cooled court bouillon over the fish. Cover with foil and steam in the oven for about 50 minutes. Remove the fish from the steamer or roasting pan and peel the skin from one side of the fish from the head to the tail, leaving the head and tail intact. Garnish the side of the fish with the almonds, using egg white to hold them in place, to give the fish a scale effect. Brown under a broiler until golden brown.

EXECUTIVE CHEF PETER McLAUGHLIN,
THE LOBSTER POUND RESTAURANT,
LINCOLNVILLE BEACH, ME

Right: sunset over Mineral Creek, Valdez. Alaskan waters provide a wealth of fish and fine seafood for the nation's kitchens.

CRAB CAKES WITH RED PEPPER AND TOMATO SAUCE

The addition of peppers and herbs makes these crab cakes especially tasty.

Preparation Time: 15 minutes
Cooking Time: 10-15 minutes
Serves: 4 as an appetizer

INGREDIENTS

1lb crab meat, picked over for shell particles
2 tbsps red bell pepper, finely chopped
2 tbsps yellow bell pepper, finely chopped
2 tbsps green bell pepper, finely chopped
2 tbsps celery, finely chopped
1 green onion, minced
2 eggs
¼ cup dried bread crumbs
1 tbsp fresh lemon thyme, chopped
1 tbsp flat leaf parsley, chopped
1½ tsps coarse salt
¼ tsp fresh ground pepper
Zest of one lemon, grated

TO COOK

Clarified butter

TO SERVE

Sprigs of lemon thyme
Corn kernels

METHOD

Combine all the ingredients, except for the lemon thyme sprigs and the corn kernels, in a large bowl and mix well. Form the mixture into cakes 1½ inches in diameter and ½ inch thick. Sauté in clarified butter over medium heat for approximately one minute on each side, or until the cakes are lightly browned.

To serve, place a spoonful of Red Pepper and Tomato Sauce on each plate. Arrange several crab cakes on top and garnish with sprigs of lemon thyme and kernels of corn.

BEN BARKER, FEARRINGTON HOUSE,
CHAPEL HILL, NC

CAPE COD MUSSELS

When seafood is as good as that from Cape Cod, even the simplest preparations stand out.

Preparation Time: 30 minutes
Cooking Time: 5-8 minutes
Serves: 4

INGREDIENTS

4½lbs mussels in their shells
Flour or cornmeal
1 cup dry white wine
1 large onion, finely chopped
2-4 cloves garlic, finely chopped
Salt and coarsely ground black pepper
2 bay leaves
1 cup butter, melted
Juice of 1 lemon

METHOD

Scrub the mussels well and remove any barnacles and beards (seaweed strands). Use a stiff brush to scrub the shells, and discard any mussels with broken shells or those that do not close when tapped. Place the mussels in a basin full of cold water with a handful of flour or cornmeal and leave to soak for 30 minutes. Drain the mussels and place them in a large, deep saucepan with the remaining ingredients, except the butter and lemon juice. Cover the pan and bring to the boil. Stir the mussels occasionally while they are cooking to help them cook evenly. Cook about 5-8 minutes, or until the shells open. Discard any mussels that do not open. Spoon the mussels into individual serving bowls and strain the cooking liquid. Pour the liquid into 4 small bowls and serve with the mussels and a bowl of melted butter mixed with lemon juice for each person. Dip the mussels into the broth and the melted butter to eat. Use a mussel shell to scoop out each mussel, or eat with small forks or spoons.

BOSTON SCROD

Scrod, or baby codfish, provides the perfect base for a crunchy, slightly spicy topping. Boston is justly famous for it.

Preparation Time: 15 minutes
Cooking Time: 12 minutes
Serves: 4

Above: Cape Cod Mussels – the heavenly taste belies the simplicity of the dish.

Facing page: Crab Cakes with Red Pepper and Tomato Sauce.

INGREDIENTS

4 even-sized cod fillets
Salt and pepper
⅓ cup butter, melted
¾ cup dry breadcrumbs
1 tsp dry mustard
1 tsp onion salt
Dash Worcester sauce and tabasco
2 tbsps lemon juice
1 tbsp finely chopped parsley

METHOD

Season the fish fillets with salt and pepper and place them on a broiler tray. Brush with butter and broil for about 5 minutes. Combine remaining butter with breadcrumbs, mustard, onion salt, Worcester sauce, tabasco, lemon juice and parsley. Spoon the mixture carefully on top of each fish fillet, covering it completely. Press down lightly to pack the crumbs into place. Broil for a further 5-7 minutes, or until the top is lightly browned and the fish flakes.

Far left: windswept Nauset Beach, Cape Cod. Massachusetts is justly famous for its many fish dishes, but few are as well known as Boston Scrod (left) — tasty baby codfish broiled in a slightly spicy breadcrumb topping.

TROUT ALMONDINE

Use the freshest trout you can find to make this simple, yet elegant dish.

Preparation Time: 30 minutes
Cooking Time: 10 minutes
Serves: 2

INGREDIENTS

2 trout, cleaned and scaled
2 cups flour
1 tsp salt
Pinch cayenne pepper
4oz (1 stick) butter
Pinch dill

Right: Smoked Tuna Salad makes an elegant and delicious luncheon salad.

Facing page: horse grooming in Delaware, a state that has an interesting cultural mix, and consequently a varied culinary tradition.

Pinch thyme
¼ cup lemon juice
2oz sliced almonds
2 tbsps white wine

METHOD

Season the flour with salt and cayenne. Roll the trout in the flour to coat. Melt the butter in a frying pan along with the dill and thyme. Sauté the trout in the butter for approximately 3 minutes, turn and continue cooking until the fish is done, about 3-4 minutes longer. When the trout is fully cooked add the lemon juice, white wine and almonds. Bring the liquid to a boil and simmer briefly. To serve, arrange the trout on a platter and pour the sauce on top.

GARY KETCHUM,
CREATIVE CULINARY SYSTEMS,
LITTLE ROCK, AR

SMOKED TUNA SALAD

Preparation Time: 15 minutes
Marinating Time: 1-2 hours
Serves: 4-6

INGREDIENTS

8oz smoked tuna
8oz can artichoke hearts, drained and quartered
½ red pepper, thinly sliced

4 leaves fresh basil, finely chopped
3 scallions, sliced
1 tomato, diced
¼ cup Extra Virgin olive oil, or more to taste
⅛ cup champagne vinegar, or more to taste

TO SERVE
Fresh salad greens

METHOD

Combine the artichoke hearts, pepper, basil, scallions and tomato. Toss lightly with the olive oil. Season with salt and pepper and gently toss again with the champagne vinegar. Allow the mixture to marinate for 1-2 hours before adding the smoked tuna. Toss lightly to combine and serve on a bed of fresh salad greens.

SUSAN PAINTER,
THE SHIP'S CABIN SEAFOOD RESTAURANT,
NORFOLK, VA

STEAMED CRABS

This is the recipe to try when you have lots of guests—and access to plenty of fresh crabs.

Preparation Time: 5 minutes
Cooking Time: 20 minutes
Serves: 20-25

INGREDIENTS

1 bushel (approximately 9 gallons) live crabs
Seafood seasoning
1 cup water
1 12oz can beer

METHOD

Place the crabs in a large steamer and sprinkle with seafood seasoning. Add the water and beer. Cover and cook for 20 minutes. Serve with French bread and a green salad.

BRICE AND SHIRLEY PHILLIPS,
PHILLIPS WATERSIDE, NORFOLK, VA

BAKED SEA TROUT IN PARCHMENT

Wrapping delicate food such as fish in paper parcels is an ingenious way of ensuring that all the flavors remain sealed in. For full effect, open the parcels at the table.

Preparation Time: 25 minutes
Cooking Time: 20 minutes
Oven Temperature: 350°F
Serves: 2

INGREDIENTS

1-1¼ lb sea trout fillet (any firm-fleshed fish will do)
4 cleaned mussels
4 Spanish onion slices

4 fresh tomato slices
4 green pepper rings
4 sprigs fresh thyme
4 sprigs fresh sage
2 crushed white peppercorns
Melted butter
White wine

METHOD

Divide the fish into two equal portions and place skinned side down on parchment paper (foil will suffice, but it is not as attractive). Garnish the fish with onion slices, tomato slices and then pepper rings. Place the mussels on top and then the herbs and pepper. Drizzle a little melted butter and wine on the fish and then seal the paper parcels, twisting the ends well. Coat the outsides with additional melted butter and bake for about 20 minutes.

THE OLYMPIA TEA ROOM,
BAY STREET, WATCH HILL, RI

SWORDFISH FLORENTINE

Swordfish, with its dense texture, is a perfect and healthful substitute for meat. Here it has a distinctly Mediterranean flavor.

Preparation Time: 25 minutes
Cooking Time: 6-8 minutes
Serves: 4

Facing page: Baked Sea Trout in Parchment, photographed at Stephen Mack's Chase Hill Farm, coastal Rhode Island.

Left: Swordfish Florentine demonstrates the Mediterranean influence in California cooking.

INGREDIENTS

4 swordfish steaks about 6-8oz each in weight
Salt, pepper and lemon juice
Olive oil
2lbs fresh spinach, stems removed and leaves well washed

AIOLI SAUCE

2 egg yolks
1-2 cloves garlic
Salt, pepper and dry mustard
Pinch cayenne pepper
1 cup olive oil
Lemon juice or white wine vinegar

METHOD

Sprinkle fish with pepper, lemon juice and olive oil. Place under a pre-heated broiler and cook for about 3-4 minutes per side. Fish may also be cooked on an outdoor barbeque grill. Meanwhile, use a sharp knife to shred the spinach finely. Place in a large saucepan and add a pinch of salt. Cover and cook over moderate heat with only the water that clings to the leaves after washing. Cook about 2 minutes, or until leaves are just slightly wilted. Set aside. Place egg yolks in a food processor, blender or cup of a hand blender. Add the garlic, crushed, if using a hand blender. Process several times to mix eggs and purée garlic. Add salt, pepper, mustard and cayenne pepper. With the machine running, pour oil through the funnel in a thin, steady stream. Follow manufacturer's directions if using a hand blender. When the sauce becomes very thick, add some lemon juice or vinegar in small quantities. To serve, place a bed of spinach on a plate and top with the swordfish. Spoon some of the aioli sauce on top of the fish and serve the rest separately.

CLAMS WITH WHITE WINE SAUCE

Preparation Time: 15 minutes
Cooking Time: 20 minutes
Serves: 4

INGREDIENTS

4 dozen clams, well scrubbed
1 cup cold water
2 tsps shallots, chopped
1 tsp garlic, chopped
4oz butter
1 cup dry white wine
Freshly ground pepper to taste
Lemon juice to taste
2 tsps fresh parsley, chopped

METHOD

Steam the clams in the water until they open, approximately 5-10 minutes. Discard any that remain closed. Place the clams in a serving bowl and strain and reserve the cooking liquid. Sauté the shallots and garlic in 2oz of the butter for about 5 minutes — do not allow them to brown. Stir in the reserved liquid and the white wine. Bring to the boil and simmer for 5 minutes. Beat in the remaining butter gradually. Do not allow the sauce to boil. Season with freshly ground pepper and lemon juice. Stir in the chopped parsley and pour the sauce over the clams to serve. Serve these delicious clams in bowls, so that guests can savor the rich sauce.

CHEF HEINZ EBERHARD.
GOURMET GALLEY. PALM BEACH, FL

Right: a Florida sunset over cypress trees near Winter Haven.

FRIED BASS IN CORNMEAL

As a coating for frying, cornmeal is superb. It fries to a crisp crunch and adds a subtle flavor of its own.

Preparation Time: 20 minutes
Cooking Time: 5 minutes per batch
Serves: 4

INGREDIENTS

2lb fresh water bass or other whitefish fillets
Milk
2 cups yellow cornmeal
2 tbsps flour
Pinch salt
2 tsps cayenne pepper
1 tsp ground cumin
2 tsps garlic granules
Lime wedges to garnish

METHOD

Mix the cornmeal, flour, salt, cayenne, cumin and garlic together in a shallow container or on a piece of wax paper. Skin the fillets if desired. Dip them into the milk and then lift to allow the excess to drip off. Place the fish in the cornmeal mixture and turn with two forks or, if using paper, lift the ends and toss the fish to coat. Meanwhile, heat oil in a deep frying pan, large saucepan or deep fat fryer. Add the fish in small batches and cook until the fillets float to the surface. Turn over and cook to brown lightly and evenly. Drain on paper towels and serve immediately with lime wedges.

Below: Fried Bass in Cornmeal.

RIVERSIDE TROUT

Brook trout is so delicious that simple preparation is all that's necessary. Crisp cornmeal, bacon and pine nuts complement the fresh flavor.

Preparation Time: 25 minutes
Cooking Time: 15-20 minutes
Serves: 4

INGREDIENTS

⅓-½ cup vegetable oil
4 tbsps pine nuts
8 strips bacon, diced
1 cup yellow cornmeal
Pinch salt and white pepper
4 trout weighing about 8oz each, cleaned
Juice of 1 lime
Fresh sage or coriander

METHOD

Heat 6 tbsps of the oil in a large frying pan. Add the pine nuts and cook over moderate heat, stirring constantly. When a pale golden brown, remove them with a draining spoon to paper towels. Add the diced bacon to the oil and cook until crisp. Drain with the pine nuts. Mix the cornmeal, salt and pepper, and dredge the fish well, patting on the cornmeal. Shake off any excess. If necessary, add more oil to the pan — it should come about halfway up the sides of the fish. Re-heat over moderately high heat. When hot, add the fish two at a time and fry until golden brown, about 4-5 minutes. Turn over and reduce the heat slightly if necessary and cook a further 4-5 minutes. Drain and repeat with the remaining fish. Drain almost all the oil from the pan and re-heat the bacon and the nuts very briefly. Add the lime juice and cook a few seconds. Spoon the bacon and pine nut mixture over the fish and garnish with coriander or sage.

BOILED MAINE LOBSTER

With today's lobster prices, it's hard to imagine that American colonists considered this delectable seafood humble and ordinary.

Preparation Time: 20 minutes
Cooking Time: 15 minutes
Serves: 4

INGREDIENTS

4 1lb lobsters
Water
Salt or seaweed
1 cup melted butter
Lemon wedges
Parsley sprigs

METHOD

Fill a large stock pot full of water and add salt or a piece of seaweed. Bring the water to the boil and then turn off the heat. Place the live lobsters into the pot, keeping your hand well away from the claws. Lower them in claws first. Bring the water slowly back to the boil and cook the lobsters for about 15 minutes, or until they turn bright red. Remove them from the water and drain briefly on paper towels. Place on a plate and garnish the plate with lemon wedges and parsley sprigs. Serve with individual dishes of melted butter for dipping.

BROILED FLOUNDER

A mayonnaise-like topping puffs to a golden brown to give this mild-flavored fish a piquant taste.

Preparation Time: 20 minutes
Cooking Time: 9-15 minutes
Serves: 4

INGREDIENTS

4 double fillets of flounder
2 eggs, separated
Pinch salt, pepper and dry mustard
1 cup peanut oil
4 tbsps pickle relish
1 tbsp chopped parsley
1 tbsp lemon juice
Dash tabasco

METHOD

Place the egg yolks in a blender, food processor or deep bowl. Blend in the salt, pepper and mustard. If blending by hand, use a small whisk. If using the machine, pour the oil through the funnel in a thin, steady stream with the machine running. If mixing by hand, add a few drops at a time, beating well in between each addition. When half the oil has been added, the rest may be added in a thin steady stream while beating constantly with a small whisk. Mix in the relish, parsley,

The elegant simplicity of Old Salem (facing page) North Carolina, as well as of dishes such as Broiled Flounder (above) reveals something of the state's European heritage.

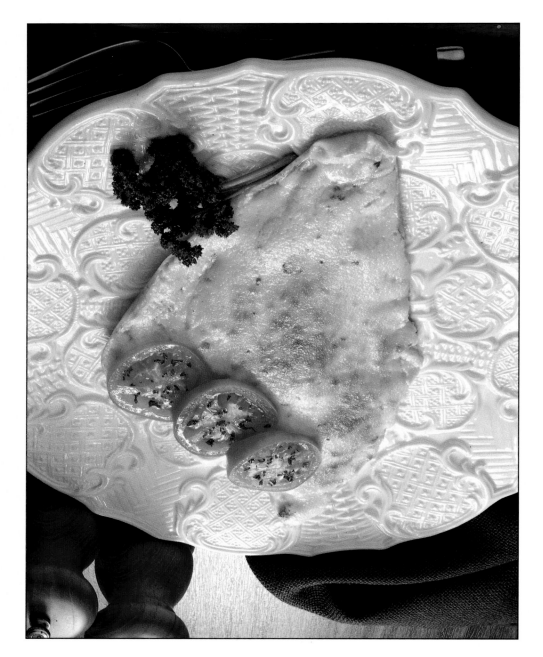

lemon juice and tabasco. Beat the egg whites until stiff but not dry and fold into the mayonnaise. Broil the fish about 2 inches from the heat source for about 6-10 minutes, depending on the thickness of the fillets. Spread the sauce over each fillet and broil for 3-5 minutes longer, or until the sauce puffs and browns lightly.

POMPANO À LA GHERARDI

This delicious fish dish is an original creation which was named for Admiral Gherardi.

Preparation Time: 45 minutes
Cooking Time: 30 minutes
Serves: 6

INGREDIENTS

6 small pompano
Salt and pepper

STUFFING

1lb cooked shrimp
½lb white crab meat
½ loaf bread
½ bunch green onions
¼ cup sherry
½ cup butter
3 tbsps parsley
1 egg

GARNISH

½lb cooked shrimp
6 strips bacon
½ cup chopped olives

METHOD

Remove the heads of the fish and split down the flat side, removing the backbone and ribs to form a pocket. Sprinkle salt and pepper inside and set aside while you prepare the stuffing.

To prepare the stuffing, mince together the shrimp, crab meat, bread, green onions, parsley and butter. Stir in the sherry and egg and season to taste with salt and pepper. Cook over a low heat, stirring frequently until heated through, about 10-15 minutes. Use this stuffing to stuff the fish. Top the pocket opening with the garnish of whole cooked shrimp, chopped olives and strips of bacon. Arrange in a covered casserole and bake at 350°F for 15 minutes, or until the fish is fully cooked.

WALTER L. SHAFFER,
HENRY'S RESTAURANT, CHARLESTON, SC
(FROM "CHARLESTON RECEIPTS,"
COMPILED AND EDITED BY THE JUNIOR
LEAGUE OF CHARLESTON, INC.)

BLACKENED FISH

Cajun cooks all have their own special recipes for the spice mixture, but all agree that the food should have a *very* brown crust when properly blackened.

Preparation Time: 20 minutes
Cooking Time: 2 minutes
Serves: 4

Left: Pompano à la Gherardi – a sophisticated dish in an equally sophisticated setting.

Facing page: Whole Baked Fish.

INGREDIENTS

4 fish fillets, about 8oz each
1 cup unsalted butter
1 tbsp paprika
1 tsp garlic powder
1 tsp cayenne pepper
½ tsp ground white pepper
1 tsp finely ground black pepper
2 tsps salt
1 tsp dried thyme

METHOD

Melt the butter and pour about half into each of four custard cups and set aside. Brush each fish fillet liberally with the remaining butter on both sides. Mix together the spices and thyme and sprinkle generously on each side of the fillets, patting it on by hand. Heat a large frying pan and add about 1 tbsp butter per fish fillet. When the butter is hot, add the fish, skin side down first. Turn the fish over when the underside is very brown and repeat with the remaining side. Add more butter as necessary during cooking. When the top side of the fish is very dark brown, repeat with the remaining fish fillets, keeping them warm while cooking the rest. Serve the fish immediately with the cups of butter for dipping.

BROILED TROUT WITH PEPPER RELISH

Fresh trout, perfectly broiled, and spicy sweet pepper relish make an unusual, innovative and very special dish.

Preparation Time: 20 minutes
Serves: 4

INGREDIENTS

1 lime
2 tbsps butter, melted
4 filleted trout, unskinned (double fillets preferred)
8 tbsps prepared hot pepper relish
Lime wedges or coriander leaves to garnish

METHOD

Remove the rind of the lime with a citrus zester and set it aside. Squeeze the juice and mix with the butter. Place the fish fillets on a broiler rack and baste with the butter and lime juice mixture. Place under a pre-heated broiler for about 4-5 minutes, depending on the thickness of the fillets. Baste frequently. Pour over any remaining butter and lime juice and sprinkle the fish with the lime zest. Gently re-heat the relish and spoon 2 tbsps down the center of each of the double fillets. Garnish with lime or coriander.

WHOLE BAKED FISH

A whole fish, perfectly cooked, never fails to impress. With a stuffing of oysters, it is certainly grand enough for an important dinner party.

Preparation Time: 25 minutes
Cooking Time: 40 minutes
Serves: 4

Right: Broiled Trout with Pepper Relish – a tasty fish dish from the Sooner State.

INGREDIENTS

4¼ lb whole fish, gutted and boned (use salmon, salmon trout or sea bass)

STUFFING

8oz savory cracker crumbs
¼ cup butter, melted
Pinch salt and pepper
2 tsps lemon juice
¼ tsp each dried thyme, sage and marjoram
1 shallot, finely chopped
10 oysters, shelled

METHOD

Have the fishmonger gut and bone the fish, leaving on the head and tail. Rinse the salmon inside and pat dry. Place the fish on lightly oiled foil. Combine all the stuffing ingredients, mixing so that the oysters do not fall apart. Open the cavity of the fish and spoon in the stuffing. Close the fish and pat out gently so that the stuffing is evenly distributed. Close the foil loosely around the fish and place it directly on the oven shelf or in a large roasting pan. Cook at 400°F for about 40 minutes. Unwrap the fish and slide it onto a serving plate. Peel off the top layer of skin if desired and garnish with lemon slices.

CALIFORNIA SHRIMP AND SCALLOP STIR-FRY

Stir-frying came to California with Chinese settlers who worked on the railroads. It's the perfect way to cook seafood.

Preparation Time: 35 minutes
Cooking Time: 8-10 minutes

INGREDIENTS

3 tbsps oil
4 tbsps pine nuts
1lb uncooked shrimp
1lb shelled scallops, quartered if large
2 tsps grated fresh ginger
1 small red or green chili, seeded and finely chopped
2 cloves garlic, finely chopped
1 large red pepper, seeded and cut into
1" diagonal pieces
8oz fresh spinach, stalks removed and leaves well washed and shredded
4 green onions, cut in ½" diagonal pieces
4 tbsps fish or chicken stock
4 tbsps light soy sauce
4 tbsps rice wine or dry sherry
1 tbsp cornstarch

METHOD

Heat oil in a wok and add the pine nuts. Cook over low heat, stirring continuously until lightly browned. Remove with a draining spoon and drain on paper towels. Add the shrimp and scallops to the oil remaining in the wok and stir over moderate heat until shellfish is beginning to look opaque and firm and the shrimp look pink. Add the ginger, chili, garlic and red pepper and cook a few minutes over moderately high heat. Add the spinach and onion, and stir-fry briefly. Mix the remaining ingredients together and pour over the ingredients in the wok. Turn up the heat to bring the liquid quickly to the boil, stirring ingredients constantly. Once the liquid thickens and clears, stir in the pine nuts and serve immediately.

Left: the awe-inspiring scenery of Cascades National Park, Washington State. The state's coastal waters, as well as her rivers, lakes and streams, provide a wealth of fish for the table.

Above: Boatman's Stew.

Facing page: an impressive and appetizing spread featuring Poached Salmon with Dill Sauce.

BOATMAN'S STEW

This quick, economical and satisfying fish dish will please any fish lover for lunch or a light supper.

Preparation Time: 20 minutes
Cooking Time: 45 minutes
Serves: 4-6

INGREDIENTS

6 tbsps olive oil
2 large onions, sliced
1 red pepper, seeded and sliced
4oz mushrooms, sliced
1lb canned tomatoes
Pinch salt and pepper
Pinch dried thyme
1½ cups water
2lb whitefish fillets, skinned
½ cup white wine
2 tbsps chopped parsley

METHOD

Heat the oil in a large saucepan and add the onions. Cook until beginning to look transluscent. Add the pepper and cook until the vegetables are softened. Add the mushrooms and the tomatoes and bring the mixture to the boil. Add thyme, salt, pepper and water and simmer for about 30 minutes. Add the fish and wine and cook until the fish flakes easily, about 15 minutes. Stir in parsley. To serve, place a piece of toasted French bread in the bottom of the soup bowl and spoon over the fish stew.

POACHED SALMON WITH DILL SAUCE

A whole poached fish is a stunning start to a meal. While looking very impressive, this salmon is easy to prepare and can be cooked ahead of time. The sauce finishes off the appetizer deliciously. A larger salmon makes a main dinner course on a warm summer evening.

Preparation Time: 25 minutes
Cooking Time: 15 minutes
Serves: 6-8

INGREDIENTS

COURT BOUILLON
2 pints water
3½oz dry white wine
½ onion, diced
2 sticks celery, diced
1 carrot, diced
1 tbsp salt
½ tsp pepper
3 whole cloves
1 bay leaf
½ lemon, sliced
3 parsley sprigs
2-3lb whole salmon, cleaned

DILL SAUCE
4 cups sour cream
3 tbsps chopped fresh dill
Juice of 1 small lemon
Pinch salt
Pinch white pepper
1 tsp horseradish

METHOD

Combine the court bouillon ingredients in a large saucepan and bring to the boil. Lower the heat and simmer for 30-45 minutes, strain and allow to cool completely. Place the salmon in a large roasting pan or a fish kettle and pour over the cool court bouillon. Cover and simmer for 15 minutes or place in a preheated 375°F oven for 15 minutes. When the dorsal fin on the back pulls out easily, the fish is cooked. Do not over-cook as the fish will continue to cook slightly as it cools. Lift the fish out of the pan and peel off the skin while still warm. Carefully transfer to a large serving plate and allow to cool. Combine all the sauce ingredients and serve with the salmon. Decorate the plate with watercress if desired.

PETER T. CROWLEY,
LA FORGE CASINO RESTAURANT,
NEWPORT, RI

STEAMED BLACK BASS ORIENTAL STYLE

Black bass abounds in the Eastern states and it is a popular fish on Rhode Island tables. For an excellent variation on the Oriental theme, the bass may be dredged in rice flour and fried in very hot peanut oil in a wok.

Preparation Time: 25 minutes
Cooking Time: 7-10 minutes
Serves: 2

INGREDIENTS

2 black bass or small sea bass, cleaned and scaled

SAUCE
¾ cup finely chopped green, red and yellow peppers
2 Szechuan peppers
1 tsp chopped garlic
1 tsp chopped fresh ginger
1 tsp fermented black beans
2 tbsps peanut oil
¼ cup dry white wine

Left: Steamed Black Bass Oriental Style, a popular Rhode Island fish given an Oriental interpretation, photographed at Stephen Mack's Chase Hill Farm, coastal Rhode Island.

METHOD

Steam the whole fish in a Chinese steamer, or improvise with a pan on a rack above boiling water, until the fish flakes easily, about 7-10 minutes. Put the peanut oil in a wok until very hot and fry the peppers until crispy. Add the remaining ingredients and cook to reduce the wine slightly. To serve, ladle over the hot fish on a serving platter.

THE OLYMPIA TEA ROOM,
BAY STREET, WATCH HILL, RI

STUFFED SOFT-SHELL CRAB IMPERIAL

This delicious dish uses some of the wonderful fresh seafood that makes Virginia famous.

Preparation Time: 30 minutes
Cooking Time: 10-12 minutes
Serves: 6

INGREDIENTS

6 soft-shell crabs

CRAB IMPERIAL MIXTURE

1lb backfin crab meat
1 egg
⅓ cup mayonnaise
¼ cup onion, finely diced
⅓ tsp Worcestershire sauce
1 tsp dry mustard
Pinch cayenne pepper

GARNISH

Parsley sprigs
Lemon wedges

METHOD

To prepare the Crab Imperial mixture first remove the crab meat from the shell carefully to keep the meat in lump form. Set aside. In a separate bowl, beat the egg and combine with the mayonnaise. Set aside a quarter of this mixture to use as a topping. Add the remaining ingredients and toss with the crab meat.

Above: dishes such as Stuffed Soft-Shell Crab Imperial have made Virginia seafood cuisine justly famous.

Facing page: yacht harbor at Newport. Fish has long been an important part of Rhode Island cuisine.

Clean the soft-shell crabs by removing the gills and viscera. Fold back the top portion of the crabs and stuff with the Imperial mixture. Bake at 350°F for 10-12 minutes. Top with the reserved mayonnaise mixture and brown under the broiler. Garnish each with a sprig of parsley and a lemon wedge. Serve hot.

BRICE AND SHIRLEY PHILLIPS,
PHILLIPS WATERSIDE, NORFOLK, VA

SHRIMP SCAMPI CANDLELIGHT

Scampi are not really shrimp but Dublin Bay Prawns or langoustines, which were once plentiful in the Bay of Naples. These shellfish are not native to American waters although shrimp, prepared in one of the same ways as scampi, makes a delicious substitute.

Preparation Time: 15 minutes
Cooking Time: 8-10 minutes
Oven Temperature: 400°F
Serves: 4

INGREDIENTS

16 large shrimp, cut down the middle, cleaned and left in their shells

SAUCE

*8oz butter, melted
2 cloves garlic, crushed
2 tbsps tarragon, chopped
2 tsps Dijon mustard
Dash A-1 sauce
Dash Worcestershire sauce
Dash Tabasco
Dash red wine vinegar
1 large tbsp sour cream
Dash lemon juice*

METHOD

Place the shrimp in an ovenproof dish and combine all the sauce ingredients. Beat well and pour over the shrimp. Cook for 8-10 minutes, or until the shrimp shells turn pink.

MARSHA HELLER, CHEF,
CANDLELIGHT INN, MA

SEAFOOD GUMBO FILÉ

Either filé powder, made from sassafras leaves, or okra gives a Cajun gumbo its characteristic texture. Gumbos are good without filé, too.

Preparation Time: 25-30 minutes
Cooking Time: 20-25 minutes
Serves: 6

INGREDIENTS

*1lb cooked, unpeeled shrimp
Half quantity spice mixture (see Shellfish Boil)
5 cups water
4 tbsps butter or margarine
1 onion, peeled and sliced
1 green pepper, seeded and sliced
2 cloves garlic, finely chopped*

Left: Shrimp Scampi Candlelight – the heavenly taste of this dish belies the speed and simplicity of its preparation.

3 tbsps flour
½ tsp thyme
1 bay leaf
2 tbsps chopped parsley
Dash Worcester sauce
12 oysters, shelled
8oz tomatoes, peeled and chopped
2 tbsps filé powder (optional)
Salt and pepper
Cooked rice

METHOD

Peel the shrimp and reserve the shells. Mix shells with the spice mixture and water and bring to the boil in a large stock pot. Reduce the heat and allow to simmer for about 20 minutes. Melt the butter or margarine and, when foaming, add the onion, green pepper, garlic and flour. Cook slowly, stirring constantly until the flour is a pale golden brown. Gradually strain on the stock, discarding the shells and spice mixture. Add the thyme and bay leaf and stir well. Bring to the boil and then simmer until thick. Add the parsley and the Worcester sauce to taste. Add the oysters, peeled shrimp and tomatoes and heat through gently to cook the oysters. Stir in the filé powder and leave to stand to thicken. Adjust the seasoning and serve over rice.

NEW ENGLAND BOUILLABAISE

French settlers brought this favorite recipe to the New World, and just as they would have at home, they used local, seasonal ingredients in it.

Preparation Time: 35 minutes
Cooking Time: 30 minutes
Serves: 4

INGREDIENTS

STOCK
1lb fish bones, skin and heads
7 cups water
1 small onion, thinly sliced
1 small carrot, thinly sliced
1 bay leaf
6 black peppercorns
1 blade mace
1 sprig thyme
2 lemon slices

BOUILLABAISE
⅓ cup butter or margarine
1 carrot, sliced
3 leeks, well washed and thinly sliced
1 clove garlic
Pinch saffron
⅓-½ cup dry white wine
8oz canned tomatoes
1 lobster
1lb cod or halibut fillets
1lb mussels, well scrubbed
1 lb small clams, well scrubbed
8 new potatoes, scrubbed but not peeled
Chopped parsley
8oz large shrimp, peeled and de-veined

Facing page: New England Bouillabaise – an American dish with French origins.

METHOD

First prepare the fish stock. Place all the ingredients in a large stock pot and bring to the boil over high heat. Lower the heat and allow to simmer for 20 minutes. Strain and reserve the stock. Discard the fish bones and vegetables. Melt the butter in a medium-sized saucepan and add the carrots, leeks and garlic. Cook for about 5 minutes until slightly softened. Add the saffron and wine and allow to simmer for about 5 minutes. Add the fish stock along with all the remaining bouillabaise ingredients except the shrimp. Bring the mixture to the boil and cook until the lobster turns red, the mussel and clam shells open and the potatoes are tender. Turn off the heat and add the shrimp. Cover the pan and let the shrimp cook in the residual heat. Divide the ingredients among 4 soup bowls. Remove the lobster and cut it in half. Divide the tail between the other 2 bowls and serve the bouillabaise with garlic bread.

SNAPPER WITH FENNEL AND ORANGE SALAD

Red snapper brings Florida to mind. Combined with another of that state's famous products, oranges, it makes a lovely summer meal.

Preparation Time: 30 minutes
Cooking Time: 6-10 minutes
Serves: 4

INGREDIENTS

Oil
4 even-sized red snapper, cleaned, heads and tails on
2 heads fennel
2 oranges
Juice of 1 lemon
3 tbsps light salad oil
Pinch sugar, salt and black pepper

METHOD

Brush both sides of the fish with oil and cut three slits in the sides of each. Sprinkle with a little of the lemon juice, reserving the rest. Slice the fennel in half and remove the cores. Slice thinly. Also slice the green tops and chop the feathery herb to use in the dressing. Peel the oranges, removing all the white pith. Cut the oranges into segments. Peel and segment over a bowl to catch the juice. Add lemon juice to any orange juice collected in the bowl. Add the oil, salt, pepper and a pinch of sugar, if necessary. Mix well and add the fennel, green herb tops and orange segments, stirring carefully. Broil the fish 3-5 minutes per side, depending on thickness. Serve the fish with the heads and tails on, accompanied by the salad.

BUTTER FISH

These are light, tasty fish caught in waters of New England Leave on the head and tail and serve them on the griddle on which they are cooked. They are delicious for breakfast with scrambled eggs.

Preparation Time: 20 minutes
Cooking Time: 3 minutes

Serves: 4

INGREDIENTS

4-8 butter fish, gutted
2-4 tbsps butter
Lemon slices

METHOD

Place 1-2 fish per person on a hot griddle with butter and cook over a low heat for about 3 minutes. The fish may not need to be turned. Garnish each fish with half a thin slice of lemon. Serve as a side dish at any meal.

STEVEN P. MACK, CHASE HILL FARM, ASHAWAY, RI

BAKED STUFFED MAINE LOBSTER

Plain or fancy, Maine lobster is superb. This "dressed up" recipe has a luxurious stuffing of crab meat flavored with sherry. Wrapping the lobster in lettuce leaves for cooking keeps it moist and adds extra flavor as well.

Preparation Time: 30 minutes
Cooking Time: 20-25 minutes
Oven Temperature: 450°F
Serves: 2

INGREDIENTS

2-3lb Maine lobster
Lettuce leaves

CRAB MEAT STUFFING

4 cups Ritz crackers, crushed
4 tbsps melted butter
½ cup cream sherry
1 tsp salt
1½ tsps Worcestershire sauce
1 drop red pepper sauce
1lb Maine crab meat

GARNISH

Lemons
Parsley
Melted butter

METHOD

Combine all the crab meat stuffing ingredients. Place the live lobster upside down on a cutting board. With a sharp knife, quickly split the lobster down the middle, being careful not to cut all the way through. Take the large claws off and remove 4-6 of the small legs and set aside. Spread the lobster apart and fill it with the crab meat stuffing. Put the lobster back together and completely cover the outside with lettuce leaves. Place in a preheated oven and cook for 20-25 minutes. If using a convection oven use the shorter cooking time. Remove the lobster from the oven, discard the lettuce leaves and arrange the small legs in an upside down V. Put the lobster under the broiler long enough to brown the stuffing. For best results, boil the claws in salted water while the lobster is cooking. Garnish with a fluted lemon half and parsley. Serve with melted butter.

EXECUTIVE CHEF PETER McLAUGHLIN,
THE LOBSTER POUND RESTAURANT,
LINCOLNVILLE BEACH, ME

Once an everyday food, lobster is now a luxury item reserved for special occasions. What better centerpiece to a celebratory dinner than Baked, Stuffed Maine Lobster (left).

AmericaCooks

CHAPTER

3

MEAT RECIPES

Previous pages: Steak over Open Fire, photographed at Stephen mack's Chase Hill Farm, coastal Rhode Island.

Below: stockyards at Dodge City, Kansas. The city has long been a railhead shipping center for cattle, supplying prime beef to the nation's markets.

STEAK OVER OPEN FIRE

Chuck steak is a much ignored and inexpensive cut that is delicious when cooked in this manner. Remove the steak just before it is done as it will cook slightly after being taken off the heat. An overcooked steak is no steak at all!

Preparation Time: 15 minutes
Cooking Time: 10-20 minutes
Serves: 4

INGREDIENTS

4 6-8oz chuck steaks, cut 1 inch thick
12-16 large mushroom caps
2 large onions, thickly sliced
Sea salt, coarsely ground

METHOD

Rub the sea salt on both sides of the meat and place on a skillet with the mushroom caps and onions. Place the skillet over a medium fire. The steaks should take only 10-20 minutes to cook, so make sure to cook them last. Turn the steaks only once while cooking and serve with the mushrooms and onions.

STEVEN P. MACK, CHASE HILL FARM, ASHAWAY, RI

MARINADED PORK LOIN WITH ORANGE SAUCE

The orange adds a refreshing tang to a succulent pork roast.

Preparation Time: 30 minutes
Cooking Time: 2½ hours
Serves: 8

INGREDIENTS

5lb loin of pork or
8 pork chops, 1 inch thick

MARINADE

½ cup lemon juice
½ cup soy sauce
½ cup red wine
½ tsp pressed garlic
2 tsps ground ginger

ORANGE SAUCE

⅔ cup sugar
½ tsp cinnamon
1 tblsp grated orange rind
20 whole cloves, tied in a cheesecloth bag
1 tbsp cornstarch

Left: Cajun Stuffed Filet Mignon, a magical mix of seafood and beef from Louisiana.

½ tsp salt
1 cup orange juice
8 orange slices, cut into halves

METHOD

Combine the marinade ingredients and pour over the pork. Cover and refrigerate overnight, turning occasionally. Remove the meat, reserving the marinade for basting. Roast at 350°F, basting often with the reserved marinade, for approximately 2½ hours, or until the meat registers 185°F on a meat thermometer. To prepare the orange sauce, combine the sugar, spices, orange rind, orange juice, cornstarch and salt in a saucepan and cook over a medium heat, stirring frequently, until the sauce is thickened and clear. Remove the bag of cloves and add the orange slices.

To serve, arrange the meat on a serving platter and pour the orange sauce over the meat.

STURDIVANT MUSEUM ASSOCIATION,
SELMA, AL

CAJUN STUFFED FILET MIGNON

Seafood and beef are combined in this recipe to make a very elegant dinner for two.

Preparation Time: 40 minutes
Cooking Time: 30 minutes
Serves: 2

INGREDIENTS

2 9oz filet mignons
¼ cup melted butter
1 tbsp crushed thyme
1 tbsp tarragon
1 tbsp sweet basil
1 tbsp rosemary
Salt and cayenne pepper to taste
¾ cup dry red wine

WHITE SAUCE

½ cup milk
1 bay leaf
1 slice onion
3 peppercorns
1 tbsp butter
1 tbsp flour
Salt and pepper to taste

CAJUN CRAB MEAT STUFFING

¾lb white crab meat
¼ cup diced onions
¼ cup diced celery
¼ cup pimentos
2 cloves garlic, chopped
¼ cup scallions, chopped
½ tsp Dijon mustard
½ tsp Pernod
1 tbsp sherry
1 tbsp fresh parsley, chopped
Salt and cayenne pepper to taste

Right: a cattle auction in progress in Oklahoma City, a major cattle center.

METHOD

Trim the excess fat and cut a ¾-inch pocket in the center of each filet. Place the meat in a roasting pan and add the butter and herbs, making sure the herbs are well distributed over each filet. Season with salt and cayenne pepper.

Next prepare the white sauce. Combine the milk, bay leaf, onion slice and peppercorns in a saucepan and bring to the boil. Remove from the heat and leave to stand for 15 minutes. In a separate pan, melt the butter and stir in the flour to make a smooth paste. Cook briefly over a moderate heat, stirring constantly. Strain the milk and gradually add to the flour, stirring constantly. Bring to the boil and simmer until the sauce is thick enough to coat the back of a spoon. Set aside to add to the stuffing.

To prepare the stuffing, combine all of the ingredients and stir in the prepared white sauce. Stuff the pockets in the meat with this mixture. Roast at 475°F for approximately 15 minutes. Deglaze the roasting pan with ¾ cup of red wine, then reduce the volume by half. Serve as a sauce over the filets.

JOHN D. FOLSE, LAFITTE'S LANDING,
P.O. BOX 1128, DONALDSONVILLE, LA

Right: Red Flannel Hash, a New England specialty that can make use of leftovers from a New England Boiled Dinner.

RED FLANNEL HASH

The name comes from the color of the dish, made bright with the addition of cooked beets. It frequently features on brunch menus.

Preparation Time: 20 minutes
Cooking Time: 25-30 minutes
Serves: 4

INGREDIENTS

1lb cold corned beef
3-4 cold boiled potatoes, roughly chopped
1 medium onion, finely chopped
Salt, pepper and nutmeg
1-2 cooked beets, peeled and diced
2 tbsps butter or bacon fat

METHOD

Cut the meat into small pieces. If using a food processor, be careful not to overwork. Combine all the remaining ingredients except the butter or bacon fat. Melt the butter or fat in a frying pan and, when foaming, place in the mixture. Spread it out evenly in the pan. Cook over low heat, pressing the mixture down continuously with a wooden spoon or spatula. Cook about 15-20 minutes. When a crust forms on the bottom, turn over and brown the other side. Cut into wedges and remove from the pan to serve.

PAN-FRIED PORK CHOPS WITH APPLE RHUBARB SAUCE

The cornmeal coating makes these pork chops crisp and tasty!

Preparation Time: 15 minutes
Cooking Time: approximately 15 minutes
Serves: 4

INGREDIENTS

4 8oz center cut pork loin chops
½ cup all-purpose flour
¼ cup stone-ground cornmeal
½ tsp salt
¼ tsp black pepper, ground
⅛ tsp cayenne pepper
⅛ tsp paprika
Peanut oil for cooking

METHOD

Combine the flour, cornmeal and spices and dredge the pork chops in this seasoned mixture until they are coated. Heat a cast-iron or other heavy-bottomed frying pan over a medium high heat for 3 minutes, then brush the pan with a thin film of peanut oil. When the oil just smokes, add the coated pork chops and reduce the heat to medium. Cook for 4 minutes, then turn the chops. Cover the pan and cook for a further 4 to 5 minutes, or until the meat is juicy, but no longer pink at the bone.

To serve, place a large spoonful of Apple Rhubarb Sauce onto a warm plate. Arrange a pork chop on top of the sauce and pour additional sauce on top.

BEN BARKER, FEARRINGTON HOUSE,
CHAPEL HILL, NC

NEW ENGLAND BOILED DINNER

The "corning process" for preserving beef was a useful one in early America. The process took a long time, but fortunately we can now buy our beef already "corned"!

Preparation Time: 30 minutes
Cooking Time: 3 hours
Serves: 4

INGREDIENTS

3lb corned beef brisket
1 bay leaf
1 tsp mustard seed

3 allspice berries
3 cloves
1 tsp dill seed
6 black peppercorns
2 potatoes, cut into even-sized pieces
4 small onions, peeled
4 large carrots, scraped
4 small or 2 large parsnips, peeled
and cut into even-sized pieces
1 large or 2 small rutabagas
1 medium-size green cabbage, cored and quartered
Salt

Facing page: Pan-Fried Pork Chops with Apple and Rhubarb Sauce. Above: the classic New England Boiled Dinner.

METHOD

Place the corned beef in a large saucepan with enough water to cover and add the bay leaf and spices. Cook for about 2 hours, skimming any foam from the surface as the meat cooks. Add the potatoes and onions and cook for about 15 minutes. Taste and add salt if necessary. Add the carrots, parsnips and rutabagas and cook for a further 15 minutes. Add the cabbage and cook a further 15 minutes. Remove the meat from the casserole and slice it thinly. Arrange on a warm serving platter and remove the vegetables from the broth with a draining spoon, placing them around the meat. Serve immediately with horseradish or mustard.

This page: the Old Foot Bridge at Harpers Ferry, West Virginia.
Facing page: Peppered Ham.

GINGERSNAP PORK CHOPS

Ginger-flavored cookies give a spicy lift to pork chop gravy, thickening it at the same time.

Preparation Time: 20 minutes
Cooking Time: 50 minutes
Serves: 4

INGREDIENTS

4 even-sized pork chops, loin or shoulder
1 tsp ground black pepper
Pinch salt
1 tsp ground ginger
¼ tsp each rubbed sage, cayenne pepper, ground coriander and paprika
Pinch dried thyme
2 tbsps oil
2 tbsps butter
1 small onion, finely chopped
1 stick celery, finely chopped
½ clove garlic, crushed
1½ cups chicken stock
12-14 gingersnap cookies

METHOD

Trim the chops if they have excess fat. Mix together the herbs and spices and press the mixture onto the chops firmly on both sides. Heat the oil in a large frying pan and, when hot, add the chops. Brown on both sides and remove to a plate. Add the butter to the frying pan and, when foaming, add the onions, celery and garlic. Cook to soften and pour on the stock. Return the chops to the pan, cover and cook for about 30-40 minutes, or until tender. When the chops are cooked, remove them to a serving dish and keep them warm. Crush the gingersnaps in a food processor. Alternatively, place the gingersnaps in a plastic bag and use a rolling pin to crush them. Stir the crushed gingersnaps into the pan liquid and bring to the boil. Stir constantly to allow the gingersnaps to soften and thicken the liquid. Boil rapidly for about 3 minutes to reduce, and pour over the chops to serve.

PEPPERED HAM

Preparation Time: 15 minutes
Cooking Time: 3½-4 hours
Serves: 8-10

INGREDIENTS

1 fully cooked or cured ham
Liquid Smoke
Sorghum molasses
Coarse ground pepper

METHOD

Trim the excess fat off the ham and rub it with Liquid Smoke and sorghum molasses. Sprinkle generously with coarse ground pepper to cover. Wrap the ham in aluminum foil and refrigerate overnight. The next day, remove the foil and place the ham in a shallow roasting pan. Bake at 325°F for 3½ to 4 hours.

LIZA, GOVERNOR'S MANSION, LITTLE ROCK, AR

BARBECUED PORK STEW

Named for the sauce rather than the cooking method, this stew requires long, slow cooking to bring out its flavor.

Preparation Time: 25 minutes
Cooking Time: 1½ hours
Serves: 4

INGREDIENTS

2lb pork shoulder, cut in 2 inch cubes
Oil
2 medium onions, cut in 2 inch pieces
1 large green pepper, seeded and cut in 2 inch pieces
1 tbsp chili powder
2 cloves garlic, crushed
1lb canned tomatoes
3 tbsps tomato paste
1 tbsp Worcester sauce
½ cup water or beef stock
2 tbsps cider vinegar
1 bay leaf
½ tsp dried oregano
Salt and a few drops tabasco sauce

METHOD

Heat about 2 tbsps oil in a large sauté or frying pan. When hot, add the pork cubes in two batches. Brown over high heat for about 5 minutes per batch. Remove to a plate. Add more oil if necessary and cook the onions and peppers to soften slightly. Add the chili powder and garlic and cook 1 minute more. Add the tomatoes, their juice and the tomato paste. Stir in the Worcester sauce, water or stock and vinegar breaking up the tomatoes slightly. Add bay leaf, oregano and salt. Transfer to a flameproof casserole dish. Bring the mixture to the boil and then cook slowly for about 1½ hours, covered. When the meat is completely tender, skim any fat from the surface of the sauce, remove the bay leaf and add a few drops of tabasco sauce to taste. Adjust salt and serve.

Far right: the annual bison round-up at Monterey, Montana, a state that boasts hearty, flavorsome fare such as Barbecued Pork Stew (right).

CHATEAUBRIAND (ROAST TENDERLOIN MADEIRA)

Hammersmith Farm has a long history. It was established in 1640 and throughout the years has been owned by just three families. Like the house and grounds where Jacqueline Bouvier had the reception after her wedding to John F. Kennedy, the recipe for Chateaubriand is truly elegant.

Preparation Time: 40 minutes
Cooking Time: 1 hour
Serves: 6

INGREDIENTS

2-3lbs beef tenderloin in 1 piece
Butter

MADEIRA SAUCE
1 cup beef consommé mixed with 2 tsps cornstarch
¼ cup dry Madeira
¼ cup butter

GARNISHES
Baked stuffed potatoes with Parmesan cheese
Small Belgian carrots
Baby onions
Asparagus
Artichoke hearts

Right: Chateaubriand (Roast Tenderloin Madeira), photographed at Rhode Island's famous and historic Hammersmith Farm.

TOMATO TIMBALES WITH BROCCOLI
6 tomatoes
6oz broccoli flowerets
Parmesan cheese
3 tbsps butter

METHOD

Fold under the thin end of the meat and tie the tenderloin at intervals with thin string. Spread the meat with butter and roast on a rack in a roasting pan for 25 minutes in a moderate oven. Cook the carrots and onions in water for about 10 minutes. Add the asparagus and artichoke hearts after 5 minutes. Drain all the vegetables and sauté them in garlic butter to finish cooking. To prepare the timbales, blanch the broccoli flowerets in boiling salted water for 2 minutes. Cut off the rounded ends of the tomatoes and scoop out the pulp and seeds. Stuff with the blanched broccoli, sprinkle with Parmesan cheese and dot with butter. Bake in a moderate oven for 10 minutes. Prepare the baked stuffed potatoes in advance and finish cooking with the tomato and broccoli timbales. When the meat and garnishes are cooked, heat the consommé and the cornstarch in a small saucepan, stirring constantly until the mixture comes to the boil. Add the Madeira and cook until slightly thickened. Swirl in the butter and serve the sauce with the Chateaubriand.

PETER T. CROWLEY,
LA FORGE CASINO RESTAURANT,
NEWPORT, RI

POT ROAST

This classic American recipe has its roots in French and German cuisine. It is an excellent way with economical cuts of beef.

Preparation Time: 30 minutes
Cooking Time: 2-2½ hours
Serves: 6-8

INGREDIENTS

3lb beef roast (rump, chuck, round or top end)
Flour seasoned with salt and pepper
2 tbsps butter or margarine
1 onion stuck with 2 cloves
1 bay leaf
2 tsps fresh thyme or 1 tsp dried thyme
1 cup beef stock
4 carrots
12 small onions, peeled
4 small turnips, peeled and left whole
2 potatoes, cut into even-sized pieces
2 tbsps butter or margarine mixed with 2 tbsps flour

METHOD

Dredge the beef with the seasoned flour, patting off the excess. Melt the butter in a large, heavy-based casserole or saucepan

Above: the fertile wheatfields of North Dakota.
Left: robust, unpretentious fare in the form of a classic American Pot Roast.

Facing page: Roast Beef Hash.

and, when foaming, brown the meat on all sides, turning it with wooden spoons or a spatula. When well browned, add the onion stuck with the cloves, bay leaf and thyme and pour on the stock. Cover the pan, reduce the heat and cook on top of the stove or in a pre-heated 300°F oven. Cook slowly for about 2 hours, adding more liquid, either stock or water, as necessary. Test the meat and, if beginning to feel tender, add the vegetables. Cover and continue to cook until the meat is completely tender and the vegetables are cooked through. Remove the meat and vegetables from the casserole or pan and place them on a warm serving platter. Skim the excess fat from the top of the sauce and bring it back to the boil. Mix the butter and flour (beurre manie) to a smooth paste. Add about 1 tsp of the mixture to the boiling sauce and whisk thoroughly. Continue adding the mixture until the sauce is of the desired thickness. Carve the meat and spoon over some of the sauce. Serve the rest of the sauce separately.

BARBECUED RIBS

No Southwestern cookbook would be complete without a barbecue recipe. This versatile sauce keeps well in the refrigerator, too.

Preparation Time: 30 minutes
Cooking Time: 1 hour 15 minutes
Serves: 6

INGREDIENTS

4½lbs pork spare ribs
1 cup tomato ketchup
2 tsps mustard powder
4 tbsps Worcester sauce
2 tbsps vinegar
4 tbsps brown sugar
Half a chili, seeded and finely chopped
Half a small onion, finely chopped
4 tbsps water
Salt (if necessary)

Right: Barbecued Ribs.

METHOD

Place the ribs in a roasting pan and cover with foil. Cook for 15 minutes at 425°F. Meanwhile, combine all the sauce ingredients in a heavy-based pan and bring to the boil. Reduce heat and simmer for about 15 minutes. Reduce the oven temperature to 350°F and uncover the ribs. Pour over the sauce and bake a further hour, basting frequently. Remove the ribs from the roasting pan and reserve the sauce. Place the ribs on a cutting board and slice into individual rib pieces, between the bones. Skim any fat from the surface of the sauce and serve the sauce separately.

ROAST BEEF HASH

Hash is a great way to use up left-over roast beef. It is a very versatile dish, too. Serve it for brunch, lunch or a light supper. Sauce Espagnole is an excellent one to have in your recipe file. It has so many uses.

Preparation Time: 25 minutes
Cooking Time: 25 minutes
Serves: 1

INGREDIENTS

1 medium potato, cooked
¼ onion
1 cup cooked roast beef, in large pieces
Pinch marjoram
Pinch thyme
Salt and pepper

SAUCE ESPAGNOLE

½ cup butter
2 tbsps celery, onion and carrot, minced
½ cup flour
1 quart brown stock
½ cup red wine
2 bay leaves
1 tsp thyme
½ tsp whole black peppercorns
1 tbsp tomato paste
1 egg, poached

METHOD

Put all the hash ingredients into a food processor and grind to a coarse consistency. Melt butter, dripping or oil in a large frying pan and when hot put in the hash mixture shaped into a patty. Brown on both sides until crisp on the outside.

To prepare the sauce, melt the butter in a large saucepan and sauté the mirepoix of celery, onion and carrot. When beginning to soften, add the flour and cook on high heat, scraping the bottom of the pan constantly, until the flour and vegetables are a golden brown. Gradually pour on the stock and add the remaining ingredients. Bring to the boil and cook for 20 minutes, until thickened. Strain and reserve. Serve the hash with a poached egg on top and some of the sauce poured around it.

MARSHA HELLER, CHEF,
CANDLELIGHT INN, MA

SEIKH KEBAB

These lamb kebabs are great cooked on the outdoor grill. In case of rain, though, they can be cooked very well under a broiler. Either way, they are sure to please.